The Complete
Beginner's Guide to
Crochet

sona
BOOKS

sona
BOOKS

First published in the UK 2019 by Sona Books
an imprint of Danann Publishing Ltd.

CAT NO: SON0439
ISBN: 978-1-912918-01-0

Made in the EU.

Welcome to

The Complete
Beginner's Guide to

Crochet

Crochet as a hobby has boomed in recent years, with
the art being passed down to younger generations.
Fashionable and thrifty, making your own garments, gifts
and decorations has become a really popular pastime.
The Complete Beginner's Guide to Crochet will show you
all the essential stitches and techniques you'll need to get
started, from your very first foundation chain to adding
embellishments like fringe and edging. Once you've
mastered those techniques, it's time to put them into
practice! Turn to the starter projects section for easy-to-
follow patterns from experienced crocheters. Start with the
rose corsage and basic bunting, then progress onto more
advanced projects like the amigurumi baby sloth. Follow
our simple steps and you'll soon be creating beautiful items
worthy of the high street. Happy crocheting!

Contents

Getting started

10	Yarns	34	Double crochet
12	Crochet hooks	36	Treble crochet
14	Crochet kit bag	38	Half treble crochet
16	Holding your hook and yarn	40	Double treble crochet
18	Crochet for left-handers	42	Turning chains
20	Tension (gauge)	44	Slip stitch
22	How to read a pattern	46	Identifying and counting stitches
24	Making a slipknot		
26	Making a yarn over	48	Fixing mistakes
27	Drawing up a loop	49	Fastening off
28	Making a foundation chain	50	Basic edging
30	Working the chain	52	Weaving in ends
32	Working into subsequent rows		

Star rating explained

Throughout this book, all crochet patterns and tutorials use UK rather than US terminology. For notes on converting between UK and US terms, head to page 23. There's also a handy list of common abbreviations on page 161 for your guidance.

The next step

56   Changing colours

58   Reading charted stitch diagrams

60   Increasing

62   Decreasing

64   Starting in the round

68   Working in the round

72   Standard increases

74   Invisible finish

76   Blocking

80   Joining

Going further

86   Shells, fans and V stitches

87   Spike stitches

88   Crossed stitches

90   Post stitches

92   Chainless foundations

94   Linked stitches

96   Cluster stitches

98   Puff stitches

100   Popcorn stitches

102   Motifs

104   Solid squares

106   Circle in a square

108   Granny squares

109   Granny triangles

110   Flower motifs

112   Fringe

114   Reverse double crochet

116   Picot edging

118   Stitch pattern gallery

Starter projects

These star ratings indicate difficulty level, so pick a pattern based on your ability:

130   Squares baby blanket
★★★☆☆

134   Teddy bear ★★☆☆☆

136   T-rex ★★★☆☆

138   Textured hot water bottle cosy
★★★★★

140   Aran cushion cover
★★★★☆

144   Traditional tea cosy
★★★☆☆

146   Spring flower brooch
★★☆☆☆

148   Lace shell-edged shawl
★★★☆☆

152   Cosy alpaca mittens
★★☆☆☆

154   Honeycomb belle hat
★★★☆☆

156   Jumbo rib scarf ★★☆☆☆

Reference

158   Glossary

161   Abbreviations

Getting Started

Get to grips with the basics of crochet

10   Yarns

12   Crochet hooks

14   Crochet kit bag

16   Holding your hook
     and yarn

18   Crochet for left-handers

20   Tension (gauge)

22   How to read a pattern

24   Making a slipknot

26   Making a yarn over

27   Drawing up a loop

28   Making a foundation chain

30   Working the chain

32   Working into
     subsequent rows

34   Double crochet

36   Treble crochet

38   Half treble crochet

40   Double treble crochet

42   Turning chains

44   Slip stitch

46   Identifying and counting
     stitches

48   Fixing mistakes

49   Fastening off

50   Basic edging

52   Weaving in ends

Yarns

From chunky wool to 4-ply acrylic, there is a wide variety of yarns with which you can crochet

To begin crocheting, all you need are two essential pieces of equipment: a crochet hook and a ball of yarn. The yarn that you decide to use will play a part in determining which hook you will work with, so let's start by looking at the many types of yarn available to you.

Yarns are made with a wide variety of fibres; most are natural, some are synthetic, and others blend different fibres together. All yarns have different textures and properties, and will affect the look and feel of your finished project. For example, wool is stretchy and tough, alpaca is soft and luxurious, while natural and synthetic blends are durable with other enhanced properties.

When choosing a yarn you also need to consider its thickness, usually called its weight. Different weights affect the appearance of your project and the number of stitches needed.

When learning to crochet, it's a good idea to start with a medium-weight yarn that feels comfortable in your hand and is smooth but not too slippery. A yarn described as worsted, Aran or 10-ply in wool or a wool blend is ideal.

Wool

Wool is very warm and tough, which makes it great for winter wear. It can be fine and soft or rough and scratchy, but will soften with washing. It's mostly affordable, durable and a good choice for the new crocheter.

Mohair

Mohair is a silk-like fibre that comes from the Angora goat. It's a yarn that dyes particularly well and is commonly blended with other fibres. It makes for fantastic winter garments as it is warm and durable.

Alpaca

With long and fine fibres, alpaca yarn can sometimes be hairy looking, but it is one of the warmest and most luxurious wools out there. It is also incredibly soft, and comes in varieties such as baby and royal, which are even softer.

Cotton

This natural vegetable fibre is typically less elastic than wool, and is known for its robustness and washability. Cotton has a lovely stitch definition when crocheted, and is good for homewares and bags. However, it can be a bit hard on the hands.

Acrylic

Made from polyacrylonitrile, acrylic yarn is both affordable and washable. This synthetic yarn is very soft to the touch and comes in a wide variety of colours and textures. Acrylic is commonly blended with other yarns in order to add durability.

Natural and synthetic blends

Blending natural and man-made fibres often creates yarns that are stronger and more versatile. It can also enhance their appearance, making them shinier or more vibrant. Blended yarns are often washable, making them great for garments for children.

Did you know?

Every ball of yarn comes with a recommended hook size, which is printed on the label. Use bigger hooks than this to make a more open stitch, and smaller ones to make a tighter, more compact fabric.

Yarn Weights

Yarn weight	Properties	Ideal for	Recommended hook sizes UK	US
Lace, 2-ply, fingering	Extremely light, Lace yarn produces a very delicate knit on 2mm (US 0) hook. Bigger hooks will produce a more open fabric.	Lace	2.25mm	B-1
Superfine, 3-ply, fingering, baby	Using very slim hooks, Superfine yarn is perfect for lightweight, intricate lace work.	Fine-knit socks, shawls, babywear	2.25-3.5mm	B-1 to E-4
Fine, 4-ply, sport, baby	Fine yarn is great for socks, and can also be used in items that feature slightly more delicate textures.	Light jumpers, babywear, socks, accessories	3.5-4.5mm	E-4 to 7
Double knit (DK), light worsted, 5/6-ply	An extremely versatile weight yarn, DK can be used to create a wide variety of things and knits up relatively quickly.	Jumpers, light-weight scarves, blankets, toys	4.5-5.5mm	7 to I-9
Aran, medium worsted, Afghan, 12-ply	With many yarns in this thickness using a variety of fibres to make them machine washable, Aran yarn is good for garments with thick cabled detail and functional items.	Jumpers, cabled garments, blankets, hats, scarves, mittens	5.5-6.5mm	I-9 to K-10 1/2
Chunky, bulky, craft, rug, 14-ply	Quick to crochet, chunky yarn is perfect for warm outerwear. Often made from lightweight fibres to prevent drooping.	Rugs, jackets, blankets, hats, legwarmers, winter accessories	6.5-9mm	K-10 1/2 to M-13
Super chunky, super bulky, bulky, roving, 16-ply and upwards	Commonly used with very large hooks, Super chunky yarn crochets up very quickly. Good for beginners as large stitches make mistakes easy to spot.	Heavy blankets, rugs, thick scarves	9mm +	M-13 +

Crochet hooks

As well as coming in a variety of different sizes, crochet hooks come in a range of styles, too. With a bit of practice, you'll find the one that suits you

Different crochet hooks are designed with various factors in mind, from the type of project you will be working on to the level of grip and comfort required. Most importantly, crochet hooks come in different sizes, and the size of hook you use — while most of the time being determined by the weight of the yarn you are working with — will determine the look of your finished project. In general, the thicker the yarn you use the larger the crochet hook you will need, but using a large hook with a fine yarn can also produce an interesting, delicate fabric.

Crochet hooks are produced in different materials — mainly metal, wood and plastic — and some come with comfy-grip or ergonomic handles. Finding the right hook for you will most likely be a matter of trial and error, but as a beginner we recommend you work with a hook that is 5mm or larger, with Aran weight yarn. This will produce defined, easy-to-see stitches that will be simple to identify and work with.

> *"Finding the right hook for you will most likely be a matter of trial and error"*

Anatomy of a crochet hook

There are six basic parts to a crochet hook, each with its own role in creating the stitches

Tip
This part can be pointy or rounded. A pointier tip will help you get into tight stitches more easily, while a rounded tip is less likely to split the yarn.

Throat
The throat of the hook guides the yarn into the working area, and catches it as you pull it through a loop of a stitch.

Grip
Sometimes also referred to as the thumb rest, this is where you grip the hook with your thumb and index or middle finger. It will often have the hook size printed on it.

Head
The head of the hook is the part that pokes into the stitch, and also comes in different styles. Inline heads are, as the name suggests, in line with the rest of the hook, whereas tapered heads have a more curved shape.

Shank
Also known as the shaft, this part determines the size of the hook, and in turn the size of the stitches that will be made with that hook.

Handle
The rest of the hook is called the handle. There are many types of handle — some are the same size as the rest of the hook, and others are larger and can be made out of more comfortable-to-hold material.

Hook sizes

Hook sizes are measured in millimetres, measured by the width across the shank. They are available from as small as 2mm to as large as 20mm or bigger. The size of hook you will need is related to the thickness of yarn that you use — thicker yarns need larger hooks — and will almost always be specified in a pattern.

Hooks can also be labelled in US sizes instead of in metric, with letters or numbers given to identify the size of the hook, as shown in the table below. If in doubt about the size of a particular hook, check the metric measurement, as this is less ambiguous.

UK size	US size
2mm, 2.25mm	B-1
2.5mm, 2.75mm	C-2
3mm, 3.25mm	D-3
3.5mm	E-4
3.75mm, 4mm	F-5
4mm, 4.25mm	G-6
4.5mm	G-7
5mm	H-8
5.5mm	I-9
6mm	J-10
6.5mm, 7mm	K-10.5
8mm	L-11
9mm	M-13
10mm	N,P-15

Hook materials

As well as varying in size and style, crochet hooks also come in a variety of materials, most commonly metal, plastic and wood — each with their own set of pros and cons. Aluminium hooks are smooth, strong and long lasting, but may feel uncomfortable in your hand after long periods of working. If you find you like the way a metal hook works with yarn but not the way it feels in your hand, you could try a metal hook with a rubber grip.

Plastic hooks are also smooth and easy to work with, but will bend more easily and could even snap. They can also make a squeaky noise when working the yarn, which could be off-putting to some. Most larger hooks are made of plastic so as to not be too heavy.

While wooden hooks feel warm to the touch, unlike cold aluminium hooks, and are flexible; they need to be well finished to ensure there are no rough spots that could snag yarn. They also need to be conditioned over time so they don't dry out. An alternative to wood is a hook made out of bamboo, which is lightweight, smooth and flexible, but prone to splintering.

To determine which type of hook is best for you, give each a try to see which feels best in your hand before you invest in multiple sizes.

Did you know?

The world's largest crochet hook was created by Jim Bolin in 2013, and is six foot 1.5 inches tall and three inches in diameter. Bolin also holds the record for the world's largest knitting needles and the world's largest golf tee.

Crochet kit bag

Although just a hook and a ball of yarn will get you pretty far in crochet, many other helpful tools are available

Case

You will only need a small case to keep all your crochet tools together, and ones designed with crochet tools in mind can be found at most craft stores. These will most likely be fitted with multiple elastic straps to keep your hooks and tools in place. However, as crochet hooks are only small, you could alternatively use a pencil case (as pictured) to keep everything in one place.

TOP TIP

If you need to use a stitch marker but don't have one to hand, a scrap of yarn tied in a loop around the stitch or even a bobby pin make pretty good substitutes.

Row counter

Row counters are used for marking off how many rows you've worked. Just turn it once when you finish a row and it will keep track for you.

Scissors

A sharp pair of scissors is one of the most important tools a crocheter can keep to hand, as you will use them frequently for cutting yarn. Try to avoid using a blunt pair as this can cause yarn to fray, making it difficult to work with.

Yarn needles

Also called a tapestry needle or a darning needle, this handy tool will be useful for finishing off your projects neatly. As these needles are thick, blunt-tipped and have a large eye to fit the yarn into, they are the perfect tool for weaving in ends and stitching pieces together, giving a professional finish to your pieces.

Stitch markers

With multiple uses, stitch markers are some of the handiest tools a crocheter can keep in their kit bag. Their main purpose is to mark stitches. Place one in the first stitch of a row so you don't lose your place in a pattern.

Fibrefill

If you need to stuff your crochet projects you will need 'toy stuffing', also known as fibrefill. You can buy it in good craft stores or simply use the innards of an old pillow!

Crocheting stuffed toys is known as amigurumi, a Japanese word meaning knitted doll. Despite this, amigurumi toys are usually crocheted.

Safety eyes

To make sure that the toys you make are suitable for children, use safety eyes as they won't come out even when tugged on!

T-pins

These are essential if you are going to block your finished pieces. While any kind of sharp pin will work for blocking, T-pins are some of the easiest to work with as they are sturdy and long. It's important to check that you're buying rust-proof pins, or else your work could be quickly ruined by rust stains.

Tape measure

A measuring device is essential for checking your gauge (tension) when crocheting. A ruler will often do, but the flexibility of a tape measure makes it easier to use. A tape measure will also come in handy if you are crocheting something to exact measurements, like items of clothing.

Holding your hook and yarn

First things first: how to hold your hook and yarn. With practice you'll find the method that's most comfortable for you

A crochet hook can feel a bit unnatural in your hand at first, but you'll soon get used to the way it feels and how it moves. If you've got a hook with a thumb rest (one without a comfort grip on the bottom), start by grabbing that part of the hook between your thumb and index finger of your right hand, with the throat of the hook facing towards you. (If you're left-handed, or you find that holding the hook in your right hand just won't work for

you, turn to the next page for our guide on crochet for left-handers). While your right hand is busy handling the crochet hook, your left hand has its own job to do — controlling the tension in your yarn. The tighter you hold the yarn in your left hand, the tighter your crocheted stitches will be, and vice versa. There are many ways you can wrap the yarn around your left-hand fingers to maintain tension, and with practice you will find a method that works best for you.

Holding your hook

There are two main ways to hold the crochet hook: overhand (knife grip) and underhand (pencil grip). Try both ways to see which feels right for you. The most important thing to keep in mind is finding a grip that will feel comfortable over a period of time.

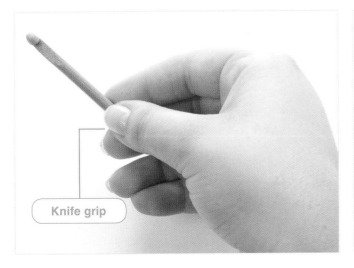

Knife grip

Pencil grip

01 Overhand

This technique is also known as the knife grip, as you grip the crochet hook as if you're holding a knife. Place your hand over the hook when you grab the thumb rest with your thumb and index finger, then support the handle in your palm.

02 Underhand

For this technique, hold the hook like a pencil (hence the name pencil grip). When you hold the thumb rest between your thumb and index finger, let the handle rest on top of your hand.

Holding your yarn

Your left hand meanwhile will be busy holding the yarn and controlling tension. Here are just two of the ways you could hold the yarn in your left hand. When you've chosen a method you're happy with, close your hand gently around the yarn to secure it in place. Make sure the yarn is not so tight that you are unable to move it through your fingers or loose enough to cause the working yarn to go slack.

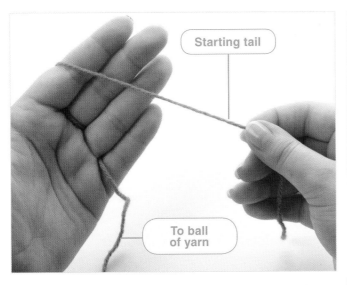

Starting tail

To ball of yarn

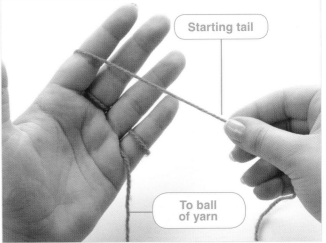

Starting tail

To ball of yarn

01 The loose-yarn hold

First, make sure you're holding the end of the yarn in your right hand, so that you will feed the working yarn to your hook. With your palm facing you, weave the yarn in front of your little finger, behind your ring finger, in front of your middle finger and behind your index finger.

02 The pinky hold

Looping the yarn once around your little finger may help you keep a more secure grip. With the end of the yarn in your right hand and your left palm facing you, begin by looping the yarn around your little finger clockwise. Next feed it behind your ring finger, in front of your middle finger and behind your index finger.

Crochet for left-handers

If you're left-handed and thinking that crochet isn't for you, don't give up just yet. There's a very simple trick to make crocheting a little easier for you...

While most crochet patterns are written for people crocheting with their right hand, it's easy to make them applicable for left-handed crocheters. As left-handed crochet produces a mirror image of right-handed crochet, there are just four instructions that need to be reversed — and these can be seen in the table on the next page. By following these simple rules, you will be able to crochet almost everything that a right-handed crocheter can with ease. The only differences will be that diagonal details slant the other way and spirals will rotate in the opposite direction, but this will rarely cause significant problems. To see what your finished piece will look like, or to follow a technique tutorial, simply hold the image up to a mirror. This will show the left-handed version.

However, there are some instances in which the mirror image will not be what you want to produce — for example, with lettering. If you simply reversed the four directions, the letters would appear back to front. In cases such as these, work from a chart by starting at the end of each row and working backwards. This should produce the results that you are looking for.

Everytime you see...	Replace it with...
Right	Left
Left	Right
Clockwise	Counterclockwise
Counterclockwise	Clockwise

Tutorials

All the tutorials in this book can be followed by left-handed crocheters. Simply follow the chart to reverse the instructions and hold the picture tutorials up to a mirror to see how you should be working.

When this is what the photo shows for a right-hander...

This is what you'd do if you're left-handed...

Tension (gauge)

When you're working to exact measurements, it's important to know how many stitches you need. Working out your tension will help with this

When creating some projects, knowing the exact size and feel of the fabric you're about to crochet before you get started will be a big help. This is where working out your tension (gauge) comes in handy. Tension is the measure of how many stitches and rows you need to create per a certain length and width of crocheted fabric. For example, crocheting tight, small stitches will inevitably result in a denser fabric than big, loose stitches will.

How tightly or loosely your crocheted stitches will be (and, ultimately, the look and feel of your piece) depends on several factors. Firstly, the size of your hook plays an important role, with a larger hook creating bigger stitches and vice versa. Secondly, the weight of your yarn will also have an impact on the end product's tension. Chunky yarns will produce denser fabrics, for example. Lastly, your own tension while crocheting will have the most unpredictable effect on any piece that you're creating. If you crochet very tight stitches, then a piece will most likely be smaller than the dimensions provided in a pattern, and it will feel thicker and more rigid than was perhaps desired.

Conversely, if you crochet very loose stitches, then the piece may be much larger than the pattern dimensions and could even appear quite holey. Working out your tension before embarking on a project can therefore save you encountering problems further down the line.

TOP TIP

Tension squares don't have to go to waste. You could keep them until you have enough to stitch together a cushion cover, or maybe even a blanket.

Creating a swatch

The easiest way to check your tension is to create a swatch with the hook, yarn and pattern you are planning to use for your project. This will give you an idea of not only whether you're making it to the right dimensions, but also what the yarn and pattern actually looks and feels like once created. The swatch should be at least 10cm (4in) in size, not including the edge stitches and rows, as these may be distorted and not provide an accurate measure. The more you crochet, the more accurate the measurements will be.

What next?

Once you have taken your measurements, compare them to the tension statement on the pattern you are using. If you have the same number of stitches, then you are ready to begin crocheting, and the dimensions of your piece should match up to the pattern. However, if you have crocheted more stitches than the tension, then your stitches are too small, and you will need to use a bigger hook to get the right tension. On the other end of the scale, if you have

crocheted fewer stitches than the tension, then your stitches are too loose and you will need to use a smaller crochet hook. If you can't quite match the tension stated on the pattern, best practice is to keep creating tension squares until you do, as this will give you the best chance of matching the pattern.

Measuring your tension

Lay out your swatch on a flat surface, taking care not to stretch it. Place a ruler or tape measure horizontally across the swatch, making sure it's placed at least one stitch away from the edge. Take a note of how many stitches there are in 10cm (4in) — this is your tension. Next, turn the ruler or tape measure vertically to measure how many rows there are within the same length, again making sure it is at least one row away from the edge. Count and take a note of how many rows there are.

Don't forget, if your finished piece is to be blocked, you will also need to block your tension square in the same way before you measure your tension, as this could have an effect on the final dimensions.

How important is it?

Obviously you won't need to make a tension square for every crochet project you do. When you're making things like children's toys or blankets, there is a bit more freedom when following a pattern. However, when creating garments to exact fitted measurements, tension squares are incredibly important, as you could find you make a piece that does not fit the intended wearer.

Ultimately, it's up to you how important the finished measurements of the piece are, and whether or not you need to check your tension with a tension square.

> "If you can't quite match the tension stated on the pattern, best practice is to keep creating tension squares until you do"

How to read a pattern

Most crochet projects are made by following a pattern. Although they may look daunting at first, they're easy to read once you understand the terms

When you've decided on what you want your first crochet project to be — whether it's a simple scarf or an amigurumi character — you will most likely follow a pattern to create it. Patterns are the instructions that tell you what stitches to use and how to combine them to make the item you're working on. You can find crochet patterns in a variety of places, including in this book (see page 128 for starter projects).

As crochet patterns are written in shorthand, to the untrained eye they can just look like meaningless lists of jumbled letters, but they're actually pretty accessible once you've mastered the terms. They are written this way so as to not take up too much space on the page, and also to make them easier to follow. Instead of a long list of words that you could easily lose your place in, patterns are concise and simple to read. All patterns should follow the same conventions, so once you've learned how to read them, any that you pick up should make sense. Read on to learn all about crochet patterns.

Starting instructions

At the top of a stitch pattern will normally be very important information that you need to know before beginning work on the pattern. This will include what size hook and weight of yarn is advised, as well as the tension. There may also be information about any special stitches you need and any uncommon abbreviations.

To begin your pattern, the first instruction will usually be to create a foundation chain (for working in rows) or a chain circle or magic ring (for working in the round). If you are not working to exact measurements laid out in the pattern, you will be told to make a foundation chain in a multiple. This is needed to ensure that any repeats don't get cut off halfway through when you come to the end of a row, as well as a small number of stitches for the turning chain. For example, 'ch a multiple of 6 sts plus 3' means you need to chain any multiple of six (6, 12, 18, 24 etc) plus three more chains at the end for the turning chain.

Rows and rounds

Crochet is always worked either in rows or rounds, and patterns give you the instructions for what you should do in each row or round you are about to create. They will be numbered (Row 1, Row 2 or Rnd 1, Rnd 2 etc) to make it easy for you to keep your place when working through the list. At the end of each instruction, the number of stitches you should have worked in that round/row will be given. If you have crocheted more or fewer than this, then you know a mistake has been made. This gives you an opportunity to correct it before you move on.

Working into specific stitches

As well as telling you which stitch to make next, a pattern will also tell you where to make it.

If the pattern says to work into the next stitch, you need to crochet into the very next stitch. For example, 'dc in next st' means double crochet in the next stitch.

If it says to work a multiple of stitches into a multiple number of stitches, you need to crochet the same stitch however many times it asks for into the number of stitches it asks you to. For example, '2 tr in next 2 sts' means make two treble crochets in the next stitch and two treble crochets in the one after it, for a total of four stitches made.

When different stitch types are given in brackets, you need to make all of the stitches given in the stitch it's asking you to. For example, '(tr, ch, tr) in next st' means make a treble crochet in the next stitch, then chain, then treble crochet in the same stitch as the first treble crochet.

If a pattern asks you to work a stitch into a specific stitch, then you skip all the ones that come before and work it into the top of the stitch it's asking you to. For example, 'dc in next htr' means double crochet in the next half treble crochet, no matter what comes before it in the row.

If a pattern asks you to work the next stitch into a chain space (ch-sp), then you need to insert your hook in the space underneath a loop that was created by a chain in the row below.

Repeats

Instead of writing out repeated instructions, they will be identified in patterns either using brackets or an asterisk (or other symbol), followed by an instruction of how many times they should be repeated within your chosen pattern.

Repeated instructions given in brackets — for example, '(2 dc in next st, tr in next st) 4 times' — means that the sequence inside the brackets needs to be followed, from beginning to end, as many times as identified by the number outside the brackets. In this case, four times.

Repeated instructions identified with an asterisk — for example, '*tr in next 4 chs, ch 2, sk next 2 chs; rep from * 3 times' — means

> ### "There is no stitch called a single crochet (sc) in UK terminology"

that the sequence that begins at the asterisk and ends at the semi colon needs to be followed, and then repeated the number of times stated. So in this case, the instruction will be followed four times.

Repeated instructions can also direct that they be worked until the end of the row, or until the last few stitches. For example, '*3tr in next st, ch 2, dc in next st; rep from * across to last 2 sts, tr in last 2 sts' means you repeat the sequence between the asterisk and semi colon until you reach the last two stitches of the row (or round), at which point you end the repeat and follow the further instructions.

Multiple sizes

A pattern may offer you multiple sizes to make something in, which is particularly common with items for infants and young children. When this happens, the information for the smallest size will be given first with the rest followed in brackets. For example,

Size: Small (medium, large)

ch 40 (48, 56)

This means that to make the smallest item, you need to follow the first instruction, for the medium size the first instruction inside the brackets and for the largest the second instruction given inside the brackets. Make sure to not use the wrong instruction, or else you may find the garment won't fit.

UK/US terminology

Always make sure you check whether a crochet pattern uses US or UK crochet terms — or you'll find yourself very confused

Follow the pattern

Confusingly, patterns that are printed in Britain and other places that follow UK naming conventions use different terms to describe stitches than patterns printed in North America. To make things even more difficult, the same name is used to mean different stitches under either convention. Most patterns will state whether they are using US or UK terminology at the start, but if not, checking the pattern's country of origin may be a good place to start in finding out which convention is being used. A handy trick to remember is that there is no stitch called a single crochet (sc) in UK terminology, so if you see this on the pattern, then you know it is using US naming conventions. Everything in this book uses UK terminology.

UK	US
Chain (ch)	Chain (ch)
Double crochet (dc)	Single crochet (sc)
Treble crochet (tr)	Double crochet (dc)
Half treble crochet (htr)	Half double crochet (hdc)
Double treble crochet (dtr)	Triple (treble) crochet (tr)
Slip stitch (sl st/ss)	Slip stitch (sl st/ss)

Making a slipknot

This easy knot is the place to start when making most crocheted items that are worked in rows

Begin to crochet
The slipknot is your first step

01 Make a loop
Wrap the yarn once around one or two of your fingers on your left hand to form a loop, making sure to leave a tail of at least 10cm (or longer if your pattern calls for it).

02 Insert your hook
Move your newly formed loop off your fingertips and grip it between your thumb and index finger on your left hand. Insert your hook from right to left into the loop.

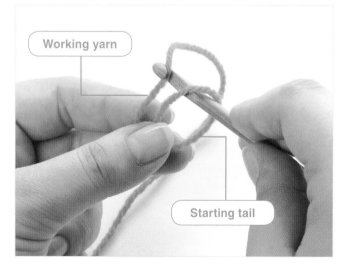

Working yarn

Starting tail

03 Identify the working yarn
The working yarn is the yarn that is attached to your ball. Catch it with your hook ready for the next step.

04 Draw up a loop
Pull the working yarn through the loop using the hook. There will now be a loop on your hook.

05 Pull it tight

Grip the tail and the working yarn between your thumb and fingers on your left hand. Pull them tight to form the knot.

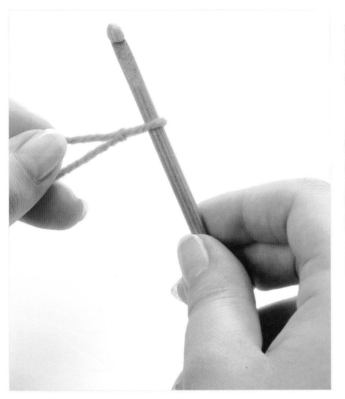

06 Close the loop...

Pull on the working yarn to close the loop around your hook. If pulling the tail tightens the knot, then you have accidentally made an adjustable slipknot, which is unsuitable. Undo your knot and start again.

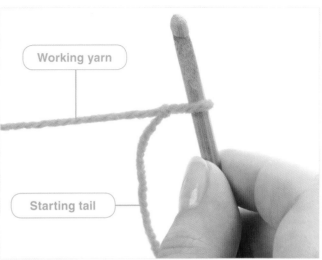

Working yarn

Starting tail

> "Leave the loop loose enough that your hook can easily slide up and down inside it"

07 ...but not too tight

While you want the loop to be tight, it still needs to be able to move up and down the hook. So ensure a small space is left around the hook when you're tightening the knot.

Leave a small space around the hook

TOP TIP

There are many different ways to make a slipknot, and if you're not happy with this one, you can experiment with a couple of others until you find a method that's comfortable for you.

Making a yarn over

This is the single most basic step in creating crochet stitches, and a technique that's important to master before moving on

The right and the wrong way
Don't let the name confuse you

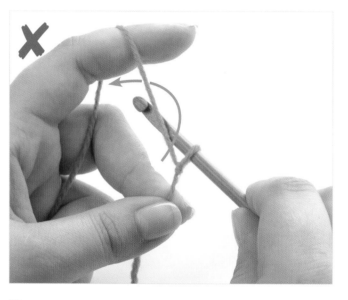

01 Move your hook, not the yarn
While it sounds like a yarn over (yo) should be made by moving the yarn over the hook, it's easier to keep the yarn still and guide the crochet hook around it. With your hook in your right hand and the working yarn in your left, pass your hook underneath the yarn from right to left.

The wrong way
Moving the hook under the yarn from left to right will make creating stitches incredibly difficult, and if you do manage it, then the stitches that you have created will become twisted and tangled.

02 Make another
There will be times when you need to yarn over twice, and to do this, just repeat the motion from Step 1, making sure to move the hook from right to left.

03 Three loops
After two yarn overs, there will be three loops on your hook: the working loop and the two that you just made by wrapping the yarn over twice.

Drawing up a loop

Everything you crochet will be formed by creating loop after loop and joining them together in different ways. Learn how to create those loops here

Making stitches
Master the basic step

01 Insert your hook
To draw up a loop, you need to insert your hook into what you've already created. This could be into the foundation chain, into a previous stitch or into a space in the work. Your pattern will tell you where.

02 Yarn over
Move your hook to create a yarn over (yo). You will always need to create a yarn over after inserting your hook to draw up a loop.

How far should you draw up the loop?
When creating basic stitches such as double and treble crochet, the loop only needs to be drawn through enough to sit comfortably on the hook. It should be identical in size to the loop already on your hook. However, there are more complex stitches that will require you to draw your loop up much taller. To do this, simply raise your hook above the work when you pull the loop through to gently tug the yarn through as much as you need to.

03 Pull through
Move your hook back through the work, making sure to catch the yarn over in the throat of your hook. There will now be two loops on your hook — the loop that you have just drawn up and the one you started with.

Making a foundation chain

When working in rows to make a piece of flat crocheted fabric, you will need to create a foundation chain to work your first row of stitches into

A solid foundation
Make your base

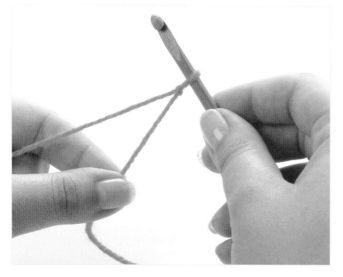

01 Start with a slipknot
The first step is to create a slipknot on your hook.

02 Yarn over
Move your hook underneath your yarn to create a yarn over.

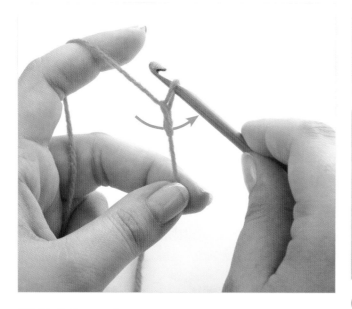

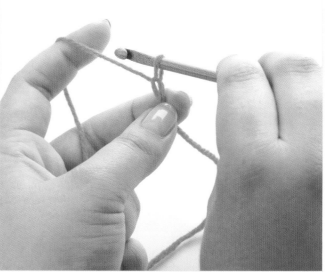

03 Pull through
Move the hook back through the loop already on your hook, making sure to catch the working yarn. You have now made your first chain.

04 Keep going
Repeat Steps 2 and 3 to make more chains. Hold the stitches you've already made in your left hand close to the hook for stability. Your pattern will tell you how many you need to chain.

Making stitches

01 Even stitches

Try to make all the chains a similar size to ensure you are making a strong foundation for your piece. If some are very loose and others aren't, the effect will be a wavy edge to your piece. This will take some practice.

02 Not too tight

It's best to keep the chains quite loose to begin with, as tight chains will be very difficult to make stitches in when it comes to the next row, as you struggle to insert your hook into them and pull it through again.

Counting chains

When beginning a project, the pattern you are following will tell you how many chains you need to create, either in total or as a multiple. It's important to create exactly the right number, as getting this wrong will mean you have to unravel your work when you find out you've either got too many or not enough at the end of your first row. To count the chains, identify the Vs on the side that's facing you. Each of these is one chain. The V above the slipknot is your first chain, but do not count the loop on your hook. This is the working loop and does not count as a chain. If you are creating a very long chain, it might help to mark every ten or 20 stitches with a stitch marker.

Did you know?

When you become more confident with crochet, you could try starting your pieces with the more advanced foundation double crochet, which creates a foundation chain and the first row of double crochet stitches at the same time.

Working the chain

Now you've made your foundation chain, it's time to get going on your project by creating your first row of stitches into the chain

Get to know the foundation chain

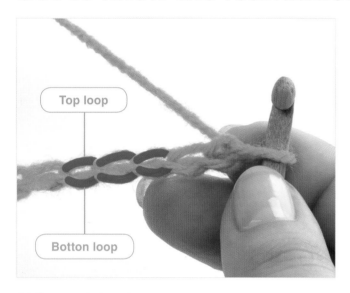

01 Front of the chain
Looking at the front side of your chain, you will see a row of sideways Vs, each with a top loop and a bottom loop.

02 Back of the chain
When you look at the back side of the chain, you will see a line of bumps in between the loops. These are called the back bumps.

Under the top loop

01 Find the top loop
For this method, hook under the top loop only.

02 Insert your hook
Move your hook to insert it under the top loop of a V.

Under the top loop and back bump

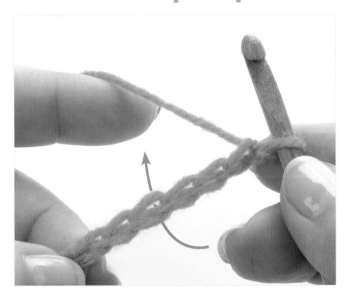

01 Under two
Hooking under both the top loop and the back bump is sometimes referred to as the top two loops of the chain.

02 Insert your hook
Move your hook to insert it under the back bump and top loop of a chain.

Under the back bump

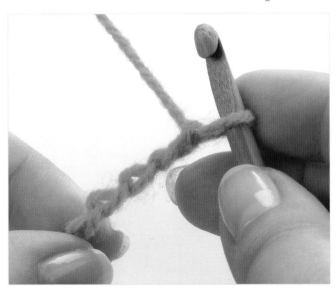

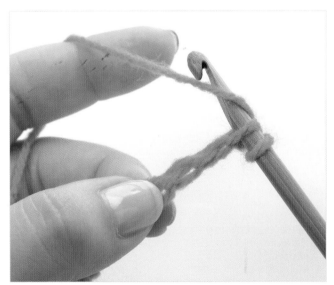

01 Find the back bump
Turn over your chain so that the back bumps are facing you.

02 Insert your hook
Move your hook to insert it under the back bump.

Be consistent
It doesn't matter which method you use as long as you are consistent when moving along the chain. Working under the top loop is the easiest method for beginners, but does not create as neat an edge as working under the back bumps. With practice you'll find the most comfortable method for you.

Working into subsequent rows

When you've completed your first row, the only way is up. The next step is to build on the row you've just worked

To work into the row you've just crocheted, you will first need to crochet a turning chain (t-ch), which you can learn how to create on page 42. When you've made this the length suggested on the pattern for the stitch that you are working, you will then crochet into the row you just created in a very similar way to working into the foundation chain.

When looking at the top of the row you will see the Vs of the stitches. To work into the next row, you can either crochet under the back loop, under the front loop or under both loops of the stitch on the row below. If your pattern doesn't specify which loops to work into, the standard way is to insert your hook under both, as crocheting under one creates a ridge along the base of the row from the unworked loops.

TOP TIP If you're struggling to find the Vs that you need to work into, skip to page 46 for more detail on how to identify and count stitches.

Under the front and back loops

Hook under the front and back loops

01 Under both
Hooking under the front and back loops of the stitch is the most common way to work into a row.

02 Insert your hook
After the turning chain (as illustrated in Step 1) insert your hook so that it goes in under both the front and back loops of the V.

Under the front loops only

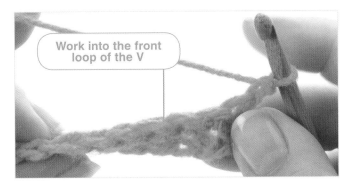

Work into the front loop of the V

01 Identify the front loop
Working into the front loop of the V only creates a ridge along the bottom of the row on the side of the work that is facing away from you.

02 Insert your hook
Make sure your hook only goes under the front loop of the V.

Under the back loops only

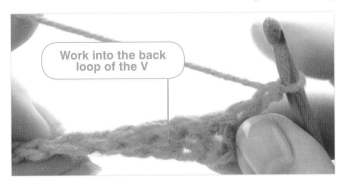

Work into the back loop of the V

01 Identify the back loop
Working into the back loop of the V only creates a ridge along the bottom of the row on the side of the work that's facing you.

02 Insert your hook
Make sure your hook only goes under the back loop on the V.

Double crochet

The easiest crochet stitch creates short and compact stitches

Double crochet (dc) is a very important stitch in crochet as it is one of the simplest, and therefore the one that most crocheters tend to learn to use first. Mastering this stitch will also help you when it comes to creating taller stitches, as most are created by just adding steps to the method for making a double crochet.

Using only double crochets creates a very compact, dense fabric, which makes it great for thick, warm winter garments. It is also a very common stitch in amigurumi and toy making, as the compact fabric created is very good for holding stuffing in. You will be able to create a variety of projects just by mastering this stitch.

If you plan to double crochet into a foundation chain, as we will in this tutorial, then you will need to make one more chain than the number of stitches you want to create, as the first stitch is never worked into the first chain from the hook. However, this will be accounted for in a pattern, so always chain the number stated.

A solid foundation
Make your base

01 Foundation chain
Make a foundation chain to the required length. If you just want to practise, start by making about 20 chains. If you want to make a piece exactly 20 stitches wide, chain 21.

02 Insert hook
Identify the second chain from your hook and then insert your hook here.

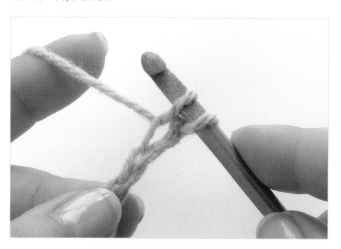

03 Draw up a loop
Yarn over (yo), then draw up a loop. You will now have two loops on your crochet hook.

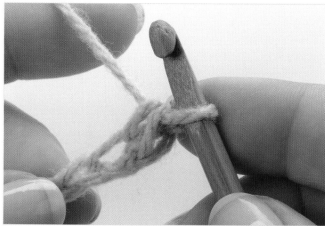

04 Pull through two
Yarn over and then draw the yarn through both loops on the hook so you have one loop left on your hook. You have completed the stitch.

05 Keep going

Continue making double crochets by inserting your hook into each remaining chain and repeating Steps 3 and 4. When you have finished the row, chain one.

06 Time to turn

Turn your work counterclockwise, so that the next stitches ready to be worked into are to the left of the hook.

Turning chain

07 Start a new row

Identify the first stitch of the row (not the turning chain). Insert your hook here.

08 Repeat

Follow Step 3 and 4 to complete the stitch.

Keep counting

Remember to count your stitches as you go along, especially when you're learning. It's easy to add in an extra stitch at the beginning or miss one off the end, and counting how many you have will alert you to a mistake at the earliest opportunity.

Treble crochet

This stitch is twice the size of the single crochet, and worked in a very similar way

The treble crochet (tr) is a very common stitch that is simple to create, especially once you've mastered the technique of making a double crochet (dc). It is created simply by adding a couple of steps to the method for creating a double crochet. Due to its increased height, this stitch creates a much less compact and therefore more versatile fabric than the double crochet. It is a very common and recognisable stitch, as seen in granny squares. When working a treble crochet into a foundation chain, you must make two more chains than your desired number of stitches. This is because a treble crochet is usually worked into the fourth chain from the hook when being worked into a foundation chain, and the three unworked chains will form your first treble crochet stitch.

Building up your skill
Make a treble crochet

01 Foundation chain
Make a foundation chain to the required length. For a precise number of stitches, chain that many plus two. Find the fourth chain from the hook.

02 Yarn over
Make a yarn over (yo) and then insert your hook into the fourth chain from the hook.hook here.

03 Draw up a loop
Yarn over, then draw up a loop. There should now be three loops on your hook.

04 Pull through two
Yarn over, then draw the yarn through two of the loops on your hook. There should now be two loops on your hook.

05 Complete the stitch

Yarn over and then draw the yarn through the two loops left on the hook. You have completed the stitch and should now have one loop on your hook.

06 Keep going

Continue making treble crochets by making a yarn over and then inserting your hook into each remaining chain and repeating Steps 3 to 5. When you have finished the row, chain three.

07 Turn

Turn your work counterclockwise ready to start the next row. The two chains you just made count as the first stitch, so your next stitch will need to be made in the second stitch of the row.

08 Continue down the row

Yarn over, put your hook into the next stitch and repeat Steps 3 to 5 to make the stitch. Continue to the end of the row, remembering to put the final treble into the top of the turning chain of the row below.

"This stitch creates a much less compact and therefore more versatile fabric than the double crochet"

Half Treble crochet

A less common stitch that is taller than double crochet but not quite as tall as treble crochet

This stitch is strange when compared to the double crochet (dc) and treble crochet (tr) in the way that it's made. Instead of drawing a loop through two loops, the yarn is instead pulled through three to create a half treble crochet (htr). This produces a stitch that's about half as tall as the treble crochet, but taller than the double crochet. This can be quite tricky to get the hang of the first time, so a little practice may be necessary. When used on its own, the half treble crochet produces a fairly compact fabric, which is similar in texture to that created when using double crochet by itself. Mastering the techniques used to create the double and treble crochet will help greatly when creating the half treble crochet.

Like with working a double crochet into a foundation chain, you will need to make one more chain than your desired number of stitches. This is because the treble crochet will be worked into the third chain from the hook, and the two unworked chains will form your first half treble crochet stitch.

Combining techniques
Make a half treble crochet

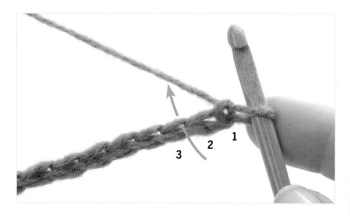

01 Foundation chain
Make a foundation chain to the required length, not forgetting to chain one more than the number of stitches you desire. Identify the third chain from the hook.

02 Yarn over
Make a yarn over (yo), and then insert your hook into the third chain from the hook.

03 Draw up a loop
Yarn over, then draw up a loop. There should now be three loops on your hook.

04 Pull through three
Yarn over, then draw the yarn through all three loops on your hook. The stitch is now complete and there should be one loop on your hook.

05 Keep going
Continue making half treble crochets by making a yarn over, inserting your hook into each remaining chain and repeating Steps 03 and 04. When you have finished the row, chain two.

06 Turn
Turn your work counterclockwise ready to start the next row. The two chains you just made count as the first stitch, so your next stitch will need to be made in the second stitch of the row.

07 Start new row
Yarn over and insert your hook into the second stitch of the row.

08 Continue to crochet
Repeat Steps 3 and 4 to complete the stitch.

Double treble crochet

This common stitch is much taller than the treble crochet, and this size allows it to be worked into a piece of fabric fairly quickly

While the other stitches you have learned create quite close, compact stitches, the double treble crochet (dtr) creates very tall stitches that make a loose, stretchy fabric. For this reason, the double treble crochet is most often found in lace work.

The double treble crochet is created by making two yarn overs (yo) before inserting the hook into the stitch or chain below, and this can make it quite fiddly to work with. It's important to check that you have the correct number of loops on your hook after you've drawn up the first loop, as it's very easy for the second yarn over to slip off the hook before you insert it into your fabric, without you even noticing. However, this is a valuable stitch because when compared to the double crochet (dc), which works up rather slowly, it's very easy to create a large piece of fabric quickly with the double treble crochet.

When creating a foundation chain to work double treble crochets into, you need to make three more chains than the desired number of stitches, as the first stitch will be worked into the fifth chain from the hook, with the four chains making the first double treble crochet hook.

The tallest stitch
Make the double treble crochet

01 Foundation chain
Make a foundation chain to the required length, making sure to chain three more than the number of stitches you need. Identify the fifth chain from the hook.

02 Yarn over twice
Make two yarn overs and then insert your hook into the fifth chain from the hook.

03 Draw up a loop
Yarn over and draw up a loop. There should be four loops on your hook.

04 Pull through two
Yarn over, then draw the yarn through two of the loops on your hook. There should now be three loops on your hook.

05 And again...
Yarn over, then draw the yarn through two of the loops on your hook again. There should now be two loops on your hook.

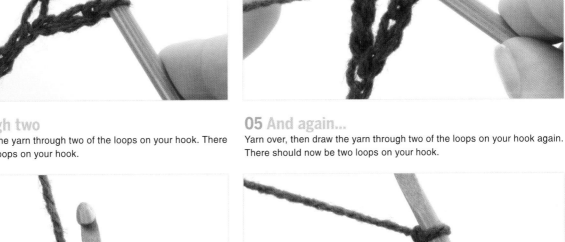

06 ...and once more
Yarn over, then draw the yarn through the two loops on your hook. There should now be one loop on your hook.

07 Complete the row
Repeat Steps 02 to 06 into each remaining chain to finish the row. When you reach the end of the row, chain four and turn your work clockwise. The chain four counts as the first stitch, so you will need to make the next into the second stitch from the end.

08 Carry on crocheting
Yarn over twice, insert the hook into the second stitch from the end of the row and repeat Steps 03 to 06 to complete the stitch.

Turning chains

At the end of every row, you need to move your hook up to the height of the stitches you are about to create. This is done using a turning chain

The turning chain (t-ch) has a very important part to play in crochet. Its purpose is to prepare for the next row to be created, and in most cases it becomes the first stitch of that row. The only exception to this is when using double crochet, as the turning chain in this case is too short to be considered the first stitch. When using anything but double crochet, the turning chain always counts as the first stitch (unless specified otherwise in a pattern), and the next stitch should be created in the second stitch from the hook. However, with double crochet, the turning chain is too short and leaving it to function as the first stitch would create messy edges, so the first double crochet is made in the first stitch from the hook. Where the turning chain does count as a stitch, don't forget to crochet into the top of it on the next row, or else your work will become smaller by one stitch every row.

> "Its purpose is to prepare for the next row to be created"

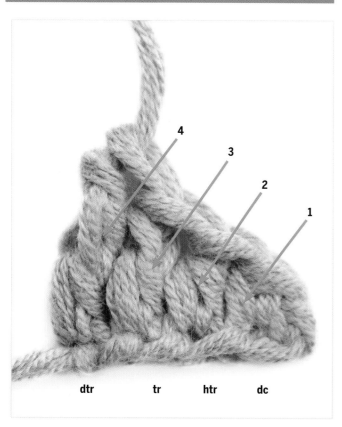

dtr   tr   htr   dc

Turning chain height

Different stitches need different heights of turning chains, which accommodates for the height of the stitch about to be made itself. However, the standard turning chain heights may not always work for you, as it depends on how loosely or tightly you create chain stitches. If you find your turning chains bulge out of the fabric, try chaining one less than specified. Alternatively, if they are tight and distorting the edge of the fabric, try chaining one more than specified. Use the table to find the standard turning chain lengths for basic stitches.

Stitch (UK)	Number of turning chains
Double crochet (dc)	1
Half treble crochet (htr)	2
Treble crochet (tr)	3
Double treble crochet (dtr)	4

Crochet into a turning chain
Prepare for the next row to be created

Did you know?
Even though it's called a turning chain, you may not always be required to turn your work after creating it. This is especially true when working in the round.

01 Identify top of turning chain
The top of the turning chain is the V attached to the last stitch you just worked into.

Back bump

Back loop

02 Insert your hook
To crochet into the top of the turning chain, insert your hook under the back loop and the back bump, then make your stitch. Don't forget to make any yarn overs needed for your stitch before inserting your hook.

Slip stitch

While rarely used on its own to create a pattern, this versatile stitch is really handy for joining stitches and moving the position of the hook and yarn without adding height

The treble crochet (tr) is a very common stitch that is simple to create, especially once you've mastered the technique of making a double crochet (dc). It is created simply by adding a couple of steps to the method for creating a double crochet. Due to its increased height, this stitch creates a much less compact and therefore more versatile fabric than the double crochet.

It is a very common and recognisable stitch, as seen in granny squares. When working a treble crochet into a foundation chain, you must make two more chains than your desired number of stitches. This is because a treble crochet is usually worked into the fourth chain from the hook when being worked into a foundation chain, and the three unworked chains will form your first treble crochet stitch.

Function over style
Make the slip stitch (sl st)

01 Foundation chain
Make a foundation chain to the required length. For a precise number of stitches, chain that many plus one. Identify the second chain from your hook.

02 Into chain
Insert your hook into the second chain from the hook. Yarn over (yo).

03 Draw up a loop
Pull your hook back through the chain. There should be two loops on your hook.

04 Pull through
Avoiding the urge to yarn over, continue to pull the yarn through the second loop on the hook. You have completed the stitch and should have one loop on your hook. Repeat Steps 02 to 04 to finish the row.

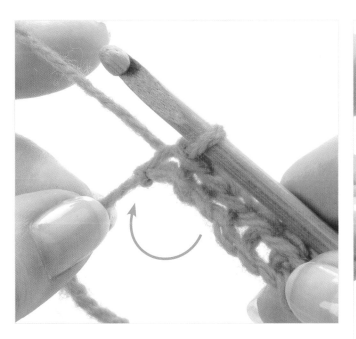

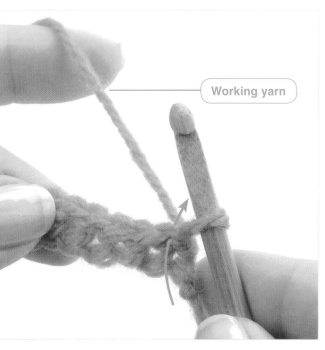

05 Turn clockwise

There will be very few instances in which you need to crochet more than one row of slip stitches. However, if you do, begin by turning the yarn clockwise when you reach the end of the row, so the working yarn is towards the back.

06 Which stitch?

There's no turning chain with a slip stitch, so you will need to make your first stitch into the first stitch of the row.

08 Continue

Repeat Steps 03 and 04 to make the slip stitch.

07 Front or back

Your pattern should specify whether to make your next stitch in the front or back loop of the stitch, as slip stitch is rarely worked under both loops. Insert your hook under the loop specified in your pattern.

> *"There will be very few instances in which you need to crochet more than one row of slip stitches"*

Identifying and counting stitches

All crocheted fabric is made up of different kinds of stitches, but learning what those stitches look like on their own is essential to creating your own work

With the guides in this book you will already have discovered how to create a foundation chain, as well as different kinds of stitches like double crochet (dc), treble crochet (tr) and half treble crochet (htr). While it is important to know how to create these stitches, it is also necessary to know what those stitches look like in your work so that you know how to count and build upon them. It can be daunting at first to look at what you've crocheted and to try to count the stitches you have just made, however if you follow these simple steps you'll see just what your fabric is made of.

Identifying stitches

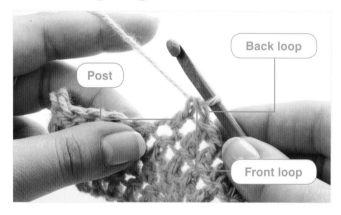

Each stitch is made up of a post (which differs in height depending on the stitch worked) and a V (which consists of a front loop and a back loop). The V sits slightly to the right of the post.

The Vs are the stitches most commonly worked into. If you turn your work at the end of a row, the Vs that you work into will be pointing to the left. Insert your hook underneath the V that is slightly to the left of the post.

If you do not turn your work at the end of each row (for example if you're working in the round), then the Vs that you will be working into will point to the right. In this instance, insert your hook underneath the V that is sat slightly to the right of the post.

Counting chains

There are two ways to count stitches: either by counting the Vs along the top of the work or by counting the posts. If you count the Vs, make sure you never count the loop that is on your hook. When counting either Vs or posts, you must take careful consideration when you come to the turning chain. If it is counted as a stitch in your pattern, then count it, but if not, leave it out.

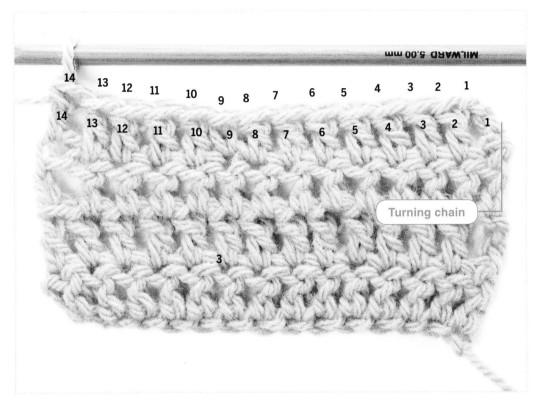

Turning chain

Counting rows

1 row

2 rows

3 rows

Counting the posts is the easiest way to count how many rows you've crocheted. When working with tall stitches, such as those made by a treble crochet, these will be easy to identify and count no matter how you're working with them. However, when working with shorter stitches, such as those made by a double crochet, the stitches can look different depending on whether you're turning your work or not.

When using double crochet in rows and turning your work, what looks like one distinct post is actually made up of two rows, as you're seeing the front and the back of the stitch. This makes it easier to count them in twos.

When using double crochet and working in the round, the stitches are more distinct as you're only seeing the front of the stitch in every round. This makes them much easier to count in single rounds.

> *"Counting the posts is the easiest way to count how many rows you've crocheted"*

Fixing mistakes

A benefit of crochet is how easy it is to undo mistakes — all you have to do is unravel to the point where you messed up, then make it right!

One of the joys of crochet patterns is that they are designed to help you identify a mistake at the earliest possible opportunity. If the number of stitches you've crocheted doesn't match the number at the end of the row on the pattern, you know that you've made a mistake. It's also quite easy to crochet one stitch when you actually meant to make another, especially if you are changing between two or more in the same row.

Luckily, mistakes in crochet are easy to fix, and if you catch them early enough, they won't set you back too much at all. Here's a look at how to fix mistakes and get yourself back on track.

Don't panic
Let's fix that mistake

Did you know?

Unravelling work is called frogging because you 'rip it, rip it, rip it', which sounds a bit like the noise a frog makes…

01 Remove hook
When you notice that things have gone awry, take your hook out of the working loop and grab hold of the working yarn.

02 Unravel
Pull on the working yarn to unravel the stitches one by one. This process is also known as frogging.

03 Find the mistake
Keep pulling the working yarn until you've unravelled the mistake. Stop pulling just after you've removed it.

04 Resume
Insert your hook into the working loop and begin redoing the work you've just undone, but this time without the mistake!

Fastening off

When you've finished a project, prevent it from unravelling by fastening off

To prevent all your hard work from going to waste and unravelling before your eyes, one of the most important steps in a project is fastening off. This incredibly simple step will lock your work in place and keep all the stitches secure. Unless otherwise stated in your pattern, always fasten off your work when you come to the end of the instructions and the piece is complete.

> *"This incredibly simple step will lock your work in place and keep the stitches secure"*

Finishing touches
Fasten off to complete

01 Cut the yarn
When you've finished your project, cut the working yarn about 15cm (6in) from the last stitch (or longer if your pattern states). Yarn over (yo) with the tail.

02 Pull through
Pull the yarn through the loop on your hook, and keep pulling until the cut end goes through the loop.

03 Pull tight
Grab the tail and pull it tight, to close the last loop. Your stitches are secure.

Basic edging

When you've finished working a flat piece, a simple border made of double crochets will help straighten the sides and give a neat finish

You may find that the edges of a flat piece of crochet worked in rows can tend to become very wavy or unattractively distorted. This happens to all crocheters at some point, and it is most likely caused by fluctuating tension. But not to worry, there's a simple solution that will give you crisp, neat edges every single time — adding a border of double crochets. This adds a degree of uniformity to all four edges, as without a border the side edges look very different to the top and bottom edges. If you simply want to neaten up your piece and create a seamless looking edge, add your border in the same colour as the rest of the work. However, a border in a contrasting colour will stand out and can add a touch of character to your work.

If your piece has a distinct front and back, make sure you add the border with the front of the piece facing you.

Function over style
Make the slip stitch (sl st)

01 Join the yarn
Insert your hook into the stitch at the top right corner of the work. Draw up a loop of the yarn you will be using for the edging, making sure to keep it tight. Chain one.

02 Double crochet
Make a double crochet into the same stitch.

03 Along the top
Make a double crochet into every stitch along the top of your work, except the last stitch of the row.

04 Make a corner

Into the last stitch of the row, make three double crochets (dc). This will keep the corner square and help it lie flat.

05 Rotate it

You will now work along the left-hand side of the piece, so rotate the work so you can work into the stitches. Insert your hook into the edge stitch (making sure it only goes under one or two loops) instead of around the entire stitch.

06 Make another corner

Work along the edge until you get to the corner. Work three double crochets into the corner stitch. Rotate the work to continue along the bottom, making one stitch in each stitch of the foundation chain.

07 Work on the next side

When you reach the end of the foundation chain, again make three double crochets in the corner stitch. Rotate and work along the side in the same way as you did for the first side.

TOP TIP

If you want to create a more decorative edge around your piece, make a double crochet border first, as this provides a stable foundation to work more stitches into.

08 Slip stitch

When you reach the last corner, make three double crochets and then join with a slip stitch (sl st) to the first stitch of the border. Fasten off. Your edging is complete.

Weaving in ends

There are several ways to hide the yarn tails and dangling ends that you'll be left with when you've finished a project

At the bare minimum, there'll always be two yarn tails that you need to deal with when you finish a project — the one at the beginning where you made your foundation chain (or started your project) and one at the end from where you fastened off. However, if you changed colour or joined new yarn, then you could be faced with many dangling ends that need to be secured and hidden away.

There is more than one right way to weave in an end, and with a bit of trial and error you'll find the one that works best for you. There are a few things to bear in mind with all methods. If your piece has a right side and a wrong side, for example a hat, then weaving in the ends along the wrong side will keep them hidden from the right side, and it doesn't matter if they get a little messy. However, if your piece will be seen from both sides, for example a scarf, a little more care needs to be taken to make sure they're hidden from both sides. Similarly, if you've worked with more than one colour, always weave the yarn into the same coloured stitches so that it blends in. Here are the most common ways to secure and hide away ends.

Sew in ends

01 Thread the needle
Thread the tail you want to weave in onto a yarn needle. Then, insert the needle through several stitches going in one direction for a few inches. Make sure the needle is passing through the middle of stitches and not underneath or over them.

02 Change direction
After a few inches in one direction, move the needle to weave the stitches in the opposite side, making sure to avoid stitches you've already weaved through. This will help to keep the yarn tail secure.

03 Check it's secure
Pull on the fabric when you are happy with the weaving in to check that nothing is coming loose and the tail is not distorting the fabric.

04 Trim it
Snip off the remainder of the tail with scissors. Pull the fabric again until the remaining tail is hidden under the last stitch you wove it through.

Crochet over ends

01 Hold the yarn

When starting a new yarn, there is an opportunity to crochet over the ends, which means they won't need to be woven in later. Hold the ends that you want to weave in over the top of the stitches that you'll be working in to.

02 Crochet over them

Continue to crochet as you normally would, but make sure to work around the tails as well so that your stitches encase them.

Weave in short ends

01 Insert a needle

If you've accidentally cut a yarn tail too short, then try this method. Pass the unthreaded needle through the stitches that you want to secure the end in.

02 Thread the needle

Pass the yarn tail through the eye of the needle when they are close together, then draw the needle all the way through the stitches.

Keep it in place

Especially slippery yarns may need a little more help to stay in place. Leaving extra long yarn tails and weaving them in in different directions will help, but you may find you need to secure them with thread or fabric glue.

The next step

Learn the more advanced techniques

56   Changing colours

58   Reading charted stitch diagrams

60   Increasing

62   Decreasing

64   Starting in the round

68   Working in the round

72   Standard increases

74   Invisible finish

76   Blocking

80   Joining

"Charted stitch diagrams lay out a pattern in a visual way, and will look similar to the actual piece of crocheted fabric"

Changing colours

Adding in different colours is a simple way to make a project look more interesting — here's what you need to know about changing colours

Colour can be used in many different ways to add a decorative element to a piece, from simple stripes to more complicated motifs and lettering. And while it might sound complicated to change colours halfway through a project, it's actually as simple as just picking up a new ball of yarn and continuing to work with it. However, it's important to remember to never start the new colour with a new stitch. Always complete the last step of the last stitch in the first colour with the new colour, as explained here. This gives a nice fluid join and makes it look like the colours flow into each other, instead of creating a harsh break.

One of the trickier elements of working with more than one colour is working with more than one ball of yarn at the same time, which means you will need to carry the working yarns that you're not using at the same time. This is often easier than cutting the yarn every time you change, as this can create lots of ends that will need weaving in at the end of a project.

Carrying yarn
Swap between colours with ease

01 Along the edge
When you're creating stripes by changing colour at the beginning of every row or so, you might choose to leave the unworked yarn dangling at the edge. That way you can pick it up again when you need to. To do this, carry it loosely up the edge of the work to begin your new row. Adding an edge or border will hide the carried yarn strands.

02 Crochet over the yarn
If you need to change colours regularly and mid-row, crocheting over the top of the yarn you're not currently using is a good way to keep it concealed. It is also there ready to use when you need to change colours without having to carry or join, eliminating ends that will need weaving in. This technique is great when you are creating a reversible fabric, as it keeps both sides looking neat.

03 Floating strands
If only one side of your work will be seen, then you can carry the unused colours along the back of the work to create loose floats of yarn. Just drop the yarn you're not using, then pick it back up again when you need it, loosely bringing it across the back of the work. This works best if the strands are only a few stitches long. If they are any longer, it may be worth cutting them and weaving them in.

04 Cutting the yarn
If you are putting in a big block of one colour, it's best to cut the yarn and treat it like you're joining a new yarn, then weaving in the ends at a later stage.

Reading charted stitch diagrams

Some crocheters find these visual representations of crochet patterns easier to follow than a written-out pattern

Made up of symbols to represent stitches, charted stitch diagrams lay out a pattern in a visual way, and will look similar to the actual piece of crocheted fabric. The symbols are uniform and internationally recognised, so you will be able to follow them with ease.

Diagrams (sometimes also called charts) can often be found accompanying written-out patterns but may also sometimes be used instead of them, especially for particularly detailed patterns such as lace work and motifs. To begin with it may be best to read a chart alongside a written pattern. Even if using a diagram becomes your preferred method of following a pattern, don't completely disregard written instructions, as these will include important information about special stitches and any repeats you may need to make.

Standard stitch symbols

The symbols for the most commonly used stitches and techniques are designed to look like the stitches they represent. The treble crochet symbol is twice as tall as the double crochet symbol, with the half treble crochet halfway between the two. The horizontal bars on the taller stitches represent how many yarn overs need to be made to begin the stitch. Use the table below to see what stitches the symbols represent:

Symbol	Stitch
⬯	ch
⬬ or ●	sl st
✕ or +	dc
T	htr
Ŧ	tr
Ŧ	dtr
◯	magic ring

Variable stitch symbols

When the basic stitches are combined to make special stitches — such as puffs, popcorns, bobbles and shells to name just a few — the stitch diagram represents this, showing the exact combination of basic stitches that is used in the pattern you are following. These may be different from pattern to pattern if the stitches are made in slightly different ways. Here are a few examples of special stitches:

Symbol	Stitch
⋀⋀	dc2tog decrease
⋀	tr3tog cluster/decrease
⬙	5-dtr shell
⬖	4-tr bobble
⬖	3-htr puff
⬖	4-tr popcorn
✿	ch-3 picot (closed)
✿	ch-3 picot (open)

> "Symbols of crochet charts have been designed to look like the stitches they represent"

Modified stitch symbols

When you need to work the next stitch into a specific part of a stitch — for example in the back or front loop only or around the back or front of the post stitch below — the stitch symbol is modified to represent this. Stitches that need to be worked into the front or back loop only include a curved symbol below them to represent this. Stitches that need to be worked around the front or back post are shown with a hook on the bottom. Foundation stitches show the stitch joined to the chain below. When stitches are crossed, the stitch that needs to go behind the other is slightly more faded than the one that sits to the front:

Symbol	Stitch
	FPtr
	BPtr
	dc in back loop only
	dc in front loop only
	foundation dc
	crossed trs

How to read a chart

Now that you have our handy reference tables to determine what all the different crochet symbols mean, you will need to know how to put them together in an actual piece of crochet. The diagram below represents the stitches as you will see them from the right side of the work (as opposed to the wrong side), and you will notice that each stitch is shown above the one that it needs to be crocheted into.

When working in rows from a stitch diagram, you almost always begin with the foundation chain and then start to work Row 1 from right to left. When you get to Row 2 if you are turning your work, you need to work from left to right. All subsequent odd rows should be followed from right to left and even rows from left to right.

When working in rounds (for example when crocheting granny squares), start from the central ring and follow the stitches in a counterclockwise direction. Do this for every round, unless an arrow at the start of the round indicates to change direction. In this case, turn the work and follow the pattern around clockwise.

> *"When working in rounds (for example when crocheting granny squares), start from the central ring and follow stitches in a counterclockwise direction"*

TOP TIP

Even rows are normally shown in a different colour than the odd rows, as this helps distinguish which stitches belong to which row.

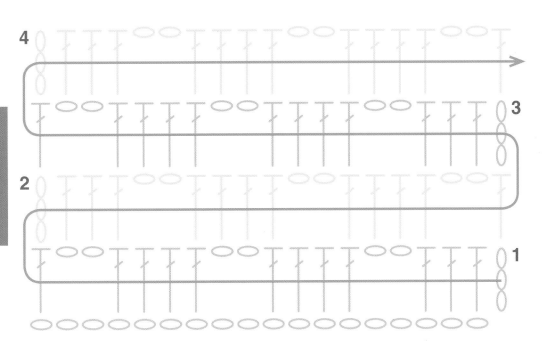

Increasing

To increase the number of stitches in a row, simply crochet two or more into the same stitch

Increasing is a very useful technique in crochet and one that's incredibly easy to execute. Increasing is essential when working in the round to create something flat, as the extra stitches add width. Without increasing, you would just build upwards, not outwards. Increasing is also very useful when shaping items — such as amigurumi — as it can be combined with decreases to make the shapes you need.

To increase the number of stitches in your round or row, simply crochet two or more stitches into one stitch of the row below. For example, if you have just crocheted a round of eight stitches, then crochet two of each stitch into each stitch below — your next round will have 16 stitches. In patterns, increasing is written as the number of stitches to be made into the stitch below. For example, '2 tr in next st'.

TOP TIP

Making lots of increases in one place will make bulges (and shells), so if you just want to make the piece larger without distorting the fabric, spread your increases out across the length of the round or row.

Adding stitches
Make a treble crochet increase in the next stitch (2 tr in next st)

01 Treble crochet
Make a treble crochet in the next stitch.

02 Into the same stitch
Make another treble crochet in the same stitch. You have increased your stitch count by one.

Increasing at the start of a row
Make a treble crochet increase in the next stitch (2 tr in next st)

01 Chain three and turn
As the turning chain normally counts as a stitch (except in double crochet), increasing at the start of a row is slightly different.

02 Into the first stitch
Where you would normally make your first stitch into the second stitch from the hook, to increase, insert your hook into the first stitch at the base of the chain and make the stitch.

03 Two stitches
The stitch you've just made and the turning chain count as two stitches, and you have made an increase.

Decreasing

Often worked in conjunction with increases when shaping crochet, decreasing stitches reduces the number of stitches in a row

While the easiest way to reduce the number of stitches in a row is to simply skip stitches, this creates a hole, which is not always the desired effect. To avoid this hole, decrease stitches work multiple stitches together, thereby eliminating stitches while also filling in the gap. Decrease stitches are named after the number and type of stitches being crocheted together. For example, 'dc2tog' means that two double crochet stitches will be combined into one. When the number in the middle increases, this means even more stitches will be crocheted into one. While decreases have many different names and forms, the basic formula is the same: make all the stitches up to the final step so that they are all on the hook, then complete all the stitches together.

Double crochet two stitches together (dc2tog)
Combine two double crochet stitches

01 Insert hook
Insert your hook into the next stitch, as if to make a double crochet. Draw up a loop.

02 Insert hook again
Without completing the stitch, insert your hook into the next stitch as if to make another double crochet. Draw up a loop. You should now have three loops on your hook.

03 Through three
Yarn over (yo) and draw the loop through all three stitches on your hook. Having worked into two stitches, but only created one, you have decreased by one.

Treble crochet three stitches together (tr3tog)
Combine three stitches

01 Insert hook
Yarn over and insert your hook into the next stitch, as if to make a treble crochet. Draw up a loop, yarn over and draw through two loops on the hook. There should now be two loops on your hook.

02 Insert hook again
Without completing the stitch, yarn over and insert your hook into the next stitch. Draw up a loop, yarn over and draw through two loops on the hook. There should now be three loops on your hook.

03 And again
Repeat Step 02 into the next stitch. There should now be four loops on your hook, for three incomplete treble crochet stitches.

04 Pull through four
Yarn over and draw the yarn through all four loops on the hook to complete the decrease. Having worked into three stitches, but only created one, you have decreased your stitch count by two.

Starting in the round

There are two options when working in the round — the most simple of which is with a starting chain

When you are working in the round you have two options for how to start your project. Usually a pattern will tell you which it would prefer for you to begin with — a chain or a magic ring, both of which will be covered on the following pages.

The most simple method to begin with is a chain, which will see you connect a short chain together into a circle and work your first round into the middle of the chain. The second method, starting with a magic ring is a little more complicated, but it produces a tighter first round, and a more secure final product. It sees you work your stitches onto a loop of yarn, which you later pull tight before proceeding to work your stitches into the round.

It should be pointed out that if you find that you prefer one method over the other, and a project suggests you use the one you aren't so keen on, it wouldn't actually affect the final product too much to use the alternate method. Do what feels most comfortable.

Single chain start
Begin your circular project with a single chain

TOP TIP
Do not work into the individual chains when starting your project with a multiple chain start. This will create a rather ugly extra first round that you don't want.

Work all the stitches into this chain

01 Make a chain
Chain two.

02 Double crochet
Now make a double crochet (dc) into the second chain from your hook.

03 Continue into the chain
Make the rest of your double crochets into the same chain stitch as your first double crochet.

Multiple chain start
Create a ring using multiple chains

01 Create a chain
Make a short chain, depending on the pattern that you're following. Here we have shown five chains.

02 Slip stitch
Create a slip stitch (sl st) into the first chain that you created.

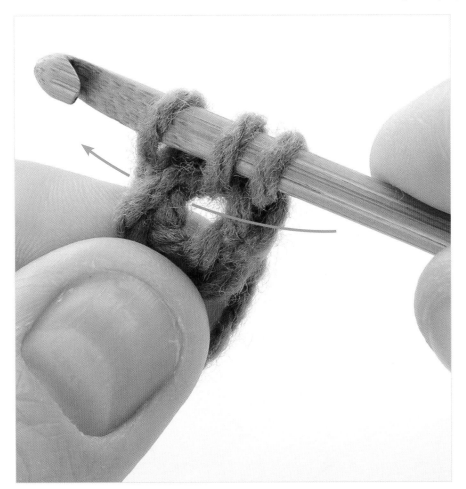

Did you know?
Crochet isn't just fun, it's good for you, too! It has been proven to help with your hand-eye co-ordination and even your maths skills.

03 Into the centre
Work your first round into the middle of the ring you have created. Now either continue to work in a spiral or connect the last double crochet to the first with a slip stitch, create your turning chains and continue on. More on this on page 68.

Magic ring
Start your project with a bit of 'magic'

01 Make a loop
To begin, create a loop (as if to create a slipknot), hold the yarn where the loop crosses over, with the starting tail in front, and insert your needle from front to back.

02 Yarn over
With the working yarn, yarn over (yo) your hook and pull up a loop back through to the front. Make sure you are not using the starting yarn — this will simply unravel.

03 Make your first stitch
Yarn over your hook again, this time from above the loop, and pull through to create a chain on your ring.

Use longer stitches
When starting with a magic ring you can create more chains in Step 03 and continue to use the extra length to use longer stitches in your project. For instance, if you want to use half double crochets (hdc) you can chain 2; chain 3 for a treble (tr); and chain 4 for a double treble (dtr).

04 Insert your hook
To create your first double crochet (dc), insert your hook into the ring, with both the loop and starting tail above your hook. Your stitches will now be created around both yarns.

05 Crochet a stitch

Yarn over and draw up a loop back to the front of the ring. Create your stitch as you would usually.

06 Keep going

Carry on with the previous two steps until you have created your ring.

07 Secure

Once you have created all of your stitches, keep your hook in the loop and hold it and your round in your dominant hand. Now pull on the starting tail until the gap is closed. Continue working as shown on page 68.

Working in the round

Following on from your chain start or magic ring, start working in the round

There are many uses for working in the round, from the most simple projects to creating brilliant crochet creations like creatures and toys. There are also various techniques you can adopt when working with this technique, from working in a continuous spiral to working in separated rounds.

Working in a spiral works best when you are working with double crochet (dc) stitches because larger stitches are harder to disguise at the end of the rounds. Having said that, if you have to do it, it isn't impossible (see example on the opposite page). At the end of your

working you will hide the last jog of stitches with an invisible finish (see page 74 for more information on these).

Working in joined rounds works well when you are using longer stitches. It consists of joining the tops of the stitches together at the end of each round, and using a collection of chains in order to create the first stitch of the next round.

Here we will show you both techniques. Your pattern may not specify whether to use a spiral or joined technique, but it will become obvious if you are asked to join each round with a slip stitch (sl st).

Continuous spiral
Keep your circular projects going in one long 'line'

Did you know?

It is theorised that crochet derives from traditional practices in Arabia, China and South America, but there is little evidence of crocheting being popular in Europe until the 19th century.

01 Crochet your round
Crochet each of your stitches into your chain start or magic ring. If you're using double crochets do six stitches, for half trebles (htr) use eight and for trebles (tr) use 12.

02 Start the next round
To start each new round, work the first stitch into the top of the first stitch of the last round. Now add your stitch marker into this stitch by slipping it through the stitch as you would crochet into it on the next round.

03 Continue your pattern
Now continue to stitch the rest of your round as stated in the pattern. Here we are doing two double crochets into each stitch.

04 Work the end of the round
Continue around until you reach the stitch before the marker you inserted earlier. This is the last stitch of the round.

05 Start the next round
To stitch your next round, remove the marker, crochet the stitch as normal and then replace the marker into the stitch you have just created.

sl st

06 Finishing your spiral
To finish your spiral you will need to smooth out the jump in stitches between rows. To do so, slip stitch into the next stitch. For taller stitches, gradually crochet shorter stitches as shown in the two images on the left.

Double crochet spiral
To end a double crochet spiral, simply slip stitch into the next stitch to hide the jog between rows.

sl st

dc

dc

TOP TIP

When using a magic ring, make sure to pull your ring tightly closed and secure it, or it will make your circle look wonky.

Treble crochet spiral
If you have worked your spiral using treble crochets, you will need to end your spiral with a half treble crochet, double crochet, slip stitch.

Working in joined rounds
Use slip stitches to join your rounds

01 Crochet your first round
Finish your first round, stitching treble crochets into your rounding ring.

02 Make a slip stitch
To join the rows, make a slip stitch into the top of the first stitch of the round — this will be as if you are creating the next stitch for double crochet — or into the top of the turning chain for any longer stitches.

03 Completed round
Now you have finished your first round and created your circle.

04 Start round two
To create your next round, create a chain to the height of your stitch. One for double, two for half treble, three for treble and so on.

Turning your work
Create different looks by turning

When you create your next rows you have the choice of turning your work or continuing on around the circle (the same as a spiral stitch). Alternatively, you can turn your work at the end of each round, and it will create a slightly different look. Apart from turning your work, you will work each of the rounds the same way.

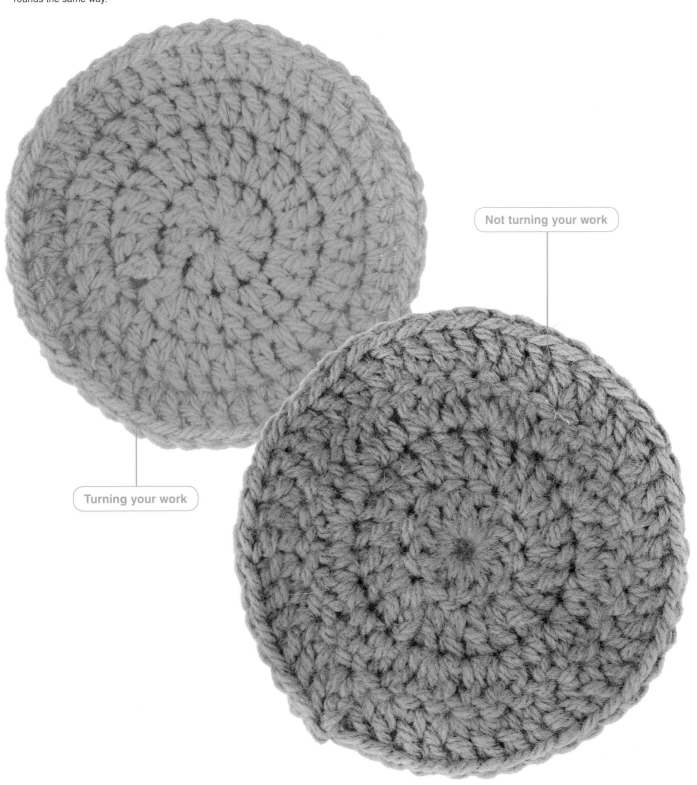

Not turning your work

Turning your work

Standard increases

When you are working in the round, you will need to learn how much to increase by each round

When you're working in the round you will need to make sure that you add a certain number of stitches to each round in order to keep your work flat (if this is the desired effect). Adding too many stitches will result in your work starting to ruffle, but not adding enough will result in a ball starting to form, which is actually perfect for amigurumi, so make sure you check the pattern if you think you have taken a wrong turn.

The number of stitches that you add per row depends on what type of stitch you have used. Refer to the table (right) to decipher how many stitches you will need to add each round.

Stitch	Stitches in first round	Increases in subsequent rounds
Double	6	6
Half treble	8	8
Treble	12	12
Double treble	18	18

Staggered increases

Keep your rounds even by staggering your increases

If you aren't careful with your increases, you will start to form straight edges on your rounds. In order to avoid this you need to ensure that your increase stitches do not stack up on top of each other. So the place to start is by simply making sure once you get into round three

that you do not start or end with your increases, but stagger them instead. For instance, start by doing one stitch, then your increase, then the rest of your stitches. On the next round do two first and so on. You can notice the improvement in the results below.

How your work will look with stacked increases.

How your work will look with staggered increases.

Double crochet

Double crochet is worked in multiples of six.

18 + 6 = 24

12 + 6 = 18

6 + 6 = 12

6

Half treble crochet

Half treble crochet is worked in multiples of eight.

24 + 8 = 32

16 + 8 = 24

8 + 8 = 16

8

Treble crochet

Treble crochet is work in multiples of 12.

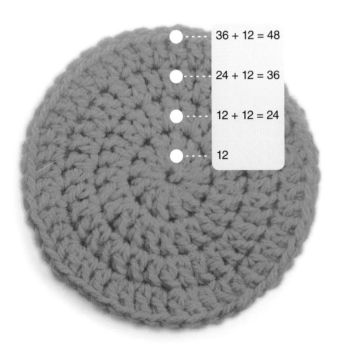

36 + 12 = 48

24 + 12 = 36

12 + 12 = 24

12

Double treble crochet

Double treble is worked in multiples of 18.

36 + 18 = 54

18 + 18 = 36

18

Check the pattern

Usually the pattern you are working with will give you instructions on how to best stagger your stitches for that particular project.

Invisible finish

Finish off your worked-in-the-round projects by hiding the yarn tail from view

When you work in the round there is nothing quite as annoying as when you can see the final stitch that joins the end of the last round to itself. Luckily, there is a very easy way to join the last stitch of your project to another stitch and create what is known as an invisible finish. To do this you will need a yarn needle (see page 14).

The invisible finish essentially sees you create your own stitch with your needle, creating a V and making it the same size and shape as the other stitches in your round. It is incredibly simple to do, and it can tie your project together by giving it a very neat finish. Doing a slip stitch (sl st) can make it look a little clunky — which is especially annoying when the rest of your project is so neat and tidy! Here we show you how to hide the end of your project.

> "It can tie your project together by giving it a very neat finish"

Invisible finish
Secure the end of your project

01 Stop crocheting
Once you have crocheted your last stitch, do not join with a slip stitch as you would have on the previous rounds if you have been working in joined rounds. Cut the yarn leaving a tail of about 15cm (6in).

TOP TIP
Do not pull your created stitch too tightly as it will be visible when you look at the finished product — which is the opposite of what you're intending to do!

02 Pull on the yarn

Carefully pull on the loop that is on your hook until the end of the tail comes thorough.

03 Thread your needle

Now get your yarn needle and thread the tail into it.

04 Insert your needle

Skip the first stitch of the round and insert your needle from front to back into the second stitch.

05 Pull through

Pull the rest of the thread through, but don't pull it tight just yet.

06 Back into final stitch

Insert your needle into the middle of the final stitch on your round. Notice that it's between the two loops, making it look like a stitch.

07 Pull it down

Gently pull on the tail until the V you've created is the same size as your other stitches. Now weave in the end of the tail.

Blocking

This step will set your flat projects into their desired shapes and give you professional results. Follow these simple but effective techniques

Blocking is a process you will go through after making many of your flat projects. It sets the stitches in place, can allow for lace pieces to become more defined and strengthens any straight edges in your work.

This, of course, means that not every piece you make will have to be blocked, but it can help to even out any variants in your tension. There are several methods for blocking, including spray, steam and wet. Each technique achieves the same goal, while, like most things, being slightly more suitable for one project over another.

To get started, you will need a blocking mat (or other flat, padded surface such as an ironing board or your bed) and some T-pins. For more fiddly projects you may want to invest in some blocking wires, which will help straighten out the edges for lace projects better than simply pinning them.

Pinning your work

Whatever the method you decide to use to block your work, the starting point is nearly always the same: pinning. Always use rust-proof pins as each of the methods requires the application of moisture to your project; if your pins aren't rust-proof they may well end up with unsightly stains on your beautiful yarn.

If you are blocking crocheted segments that are due to be joined, make sure you measure them out so they match when you come to sew them together.

To pin, lay out your piece on a flat surface, roughly in the correct shape. Start by pinning the corners to the correct measurement for your final piece. Then pin half way along the edge, and keep doing this until you are happy that the edges are all straight and even.

> "Blocking sets stitches in place and can strengthen straight edges"

Spray blocking

Spray blocking is the easiest and quickest way of blocking your work. Once you've pinned your piece into position, simply take a spray bottle and give a few sprays of water until the surface of your work is evenly coated and saturated. Now gently pat the surface to help the water absorb into the yarn fibres. Leave your work to dry; this can take up to (and sometimes over) 24 hours, depending on how much water your yarn retains, and how much water you used.

TOP TIP
Leave your project for 24 hours or more. The rate at which it dries depends on the room temperature, the type of yarn used and how much moisture was retained in the fibres.

Steam blocking

As you might be able to guess, steam blocking requires the use of an iron or handheld steamer, and uses the moisture and heat from the steam to help block your project. What you must be most wary of is not touching the iron to the yarn at any point. Man-made fibres will melt, and all your hard work will go to waste (not to mention the mess it would create for your equipment).

Pin your piece, and hold your steamer or iron about 2.5cm (1in) from the surface of your project. Steam it until the entire surface area is moist to the touch. Once you're happy, put down your steaming device and pat the surface gently in order to allow the moisture to penetrate the yarn fibres more thoroughly. Leave to dry.

As with spray blocking, this could take up to 24 hours depending on your yarn and how damp it became in the blocking process.

Wet blocking

01 Immerse in water

Fill your sink, washing-up bowl or even a bath for larger items, with lukewarm water. You can also add in some no-rinse wool wash at this stage. Immerse your project (in this case a simple swatch) in the water, pushing down until it is saturated. Leave it for 20 minutes.

02 Be gentle

Take your project from the water and gently squeeze out the excess liquid. Do not wring your project, this will stretch the yarn fibres out of shape. Continue to squeeze gently until you think you can remove no more water.

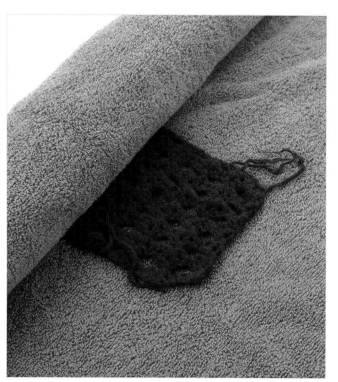

03 Grab a towel

Use a towel to squeeze out a little more moisture. Lay the towel on a flat surface (the floor is probably easiest) and lie your garment flat. Gently roll up your towel. This will gently press out even more water.

04 Pin and leave to dry

Now pin your project to your blocking surface (a foam mat or even a mattress is ideal) and leave to dry. This could take at least 24 hours depending on the fibre type.

Blocking lace

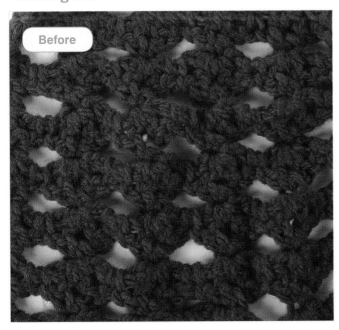

Before

After

If you have made a lace garment, such as a scarf or a cardigan, blocking your final project can really make it stand out. It will make the lace stitches more defined, and take any crumples out of the final product. You will need to start by using the wet blocking method on the opposite page, but at the pinning stage make sure you arrange your work to the dimensions stated on the pattern. You can use extra pins at this stage. You can also use blocking wires for the edges to make sure they remain crisp without having to use an excessive number of pins.

Using a wire allows you to create a really straight edge

"Blocking will make the lace stitches more defined, and take any crumples out of the final product"

Pinning your project may cause curves along the edge

01 Using a wire
For more refined edging, thread a blocking wire through each stitch or row end along the straight edge of your project. You may wish to add a few pins as you go to keep it in place.

02 Pinning
If your lace garment has straight edges you will need to use a lot of pins along the edge of a lace garment in order to obtain a professional result. It will bow in places if you don't use enough.

Joining
Finish projects that need joining together with these simple techniques

When making larger garments such as bags and items of clothing, a pattern can direct you to join pieces of crochet together. This is simple enough when it is simply attaching a motif, but when you are seaming together two separate parts of crochet, the process can become a touch more complicated, especially if you discover that the number of stitches do not correspond with each other.

When joining pieces you do so stitch by stitch to give a clean finish. Joining a piece worked in rows can be a little more complicated because of the difficulty of working into the row edges. If the number of stitches per row doesn't correspond then you may have to work more than one joining stitch into each V or row space. It is best when joining pieces of different sizes to place stitch markers along the pieces, holding them together every 5cm (2in) or so. This way you will be able to keep your stitches spaced more evenly.

Before you join your crochet, it is best to block your project's pieces first (if it's required). Otherwise you could experience a rippling effect later if you were to block them afterwards.

Whip stitch
Join your work simply

01 Hold 'wrong sides' together
Hold two pieces together with the wrong sides facing each other (the side of the pattern not meant to face the world). Pass your needle through the V stitches on both pieces from front to back and pull the yarn through.

02 Back to the front
Instead of doing your next stitch from back to front, simply draw your needle back to the front and repeat Step 01, inserting your needle from front to back. Repeat this until complete.

03 The finished look
Using a whip stitch will leave a visible line on both sides of the piece. This won't be quite as obvious when you are using the same colour.

> "Before you join your crochet, it is best to block your project's pieces first (if it's required)"

Mattress stitch
Make your join more secure

01 Lay them down
Lay your pieces side-by-side with the right sides facing you. Leaving a tail of 15cm (6in), insert your needle through the first edge stitch of the first piece and then down through the edge of the second.

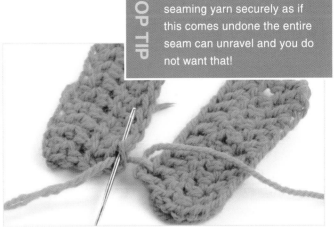

02 Through stitch
Insert your needle down through the first stitch of piece one and up through to the second stitch.

03 Same to piece two
Now repeat the same process on piece two.

04 Repeat
Keep going up the edges of your two pieces. A loose 'ladder' will start to form. Stop when you have done about 2.5cm (1in).

05 Pull together
Now pull gently on the yarn so that the rungs of your ladder draw the two sides together. Be careful not to pull too tightly as this will make the crocheted pieces buckle.

06 Keep going
Repeat until you have reached the end, pulling the yarn to draw the edges together every 2.5cm (1in) or so. Notice how the seam is almost invisible. We've used a contrasting colour to make it obvious, but when it is the same colour you'll barely know it's there!

Slip stitch
Crochet your pieces together

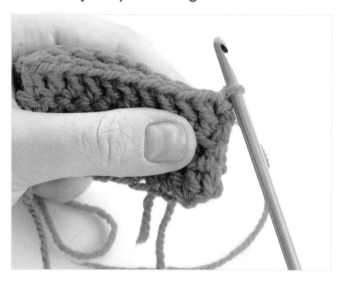

01 Slip stitch (sl st)
Insert your hook through the first stitch on both pieces of crochet.
Complete your slip stitch (or double crochet) along the edge.

02 Keep going
Now keep going, ensuring you match up the stitches as you go.

Slip stitch
A slip stitch seam is strong, and will be almost invisible from the other
side of the work. Be mindful that slip stitches do not allow for any give,
so making them too tight will pucker the fabric. Keep your tension loose
but secure.

Double crochet
Using a double crochet will give a more pronounced edge, but this can be
used to your advantage if you want a decorative seam. It is also stretchier
than a slip stitch join.

Flat slip-stitched seam
Make a flat and symmetrical join

01 Top to bottom
Insert your hook from top to bottom through the back loop only on the right-hand piece of fabric.

02 Now to the left
Do the same on your left piece, then yarn over (yo) and pull through both loops on the hook. Repeat until you reach the end.

Flat slip-stitched seam
This seam produces a flat row of chain-looking stitches. It's a neat finish and adds a nice little detail to your seams.

> "It is best when joining pieces of different sizes to place stitch markers along the pieces, holding them together every 5cm (2in) or so"

Check the name
Each of the stitches used here has another name, so it is best to be aware of these just in case the pattern you are using calls them by another name:

• Whip stitch: overcast stitch

• Mattress stitch: ladder stitch

• Slip stitch: double crochet seam

Going further

Start adding embellishments and decorative stitches

86 Shells, fans and V stitches

87 Spike stitches

88 Crossed stitches

90 Post stitches

92 Chainless foundations

94 Linked stitches

96 Cluster stitches

98 Puff stitches

100 Popcorn stitches

102 Motifs

104 Solid squares

106 Circle in a square

108 Granny squares

109 Granny triangles

110 Flower motifs

112 Fringe

114 Reverse double crochet

116 Picot edging

118 Stitch pattern gallery

"In crochet, a motif is any sort of smaller piece of crochet you create that's intended to be part of a bigger project"

Shells, fans and V stitches
Create better edges with these three decorative embellishments

In crochet, the terms shell and fan are used interchangeably, but in actual fact they are not quite the same. Where a shell sees you use a solid run of stitches, a fan will utilise the added gap of a chain space (ch-sp). Meanwhile, the V stitch uses fewer stitches, and comprises two stitches in the same stitch, separated by a chain. The result is a singular chain space. Shells and fans typically use five stitches into the same stitch. They are best used with treble (tr) or double treble (dtr) stitches as this makes them more prominent.

Below are some examples of how each of these would be worked, and what the end product would look like.

> *"Where a shell sees you use a solid run of stitches, a fan will utilise the added gap of a chain space"*

Shell
Skip the next stitch, 5 treble into next stitch, skip stitch, continue with pattern.

Fan
Skip the next stitch, (treble, chain (ch) 1, treble, chain 1, treble) into next stitch, skip stitch, continue with pattern.

V stitch
Skip the next stitch, (treble, chain 1, treble) into next stitch, skip stitch, continue with pattern.

Spike stitches

Add texture and detail to your piece with the simple spike stitch

One of the best things about crochet is that you don't have to do much in order to add an extra little flourish to your work. It's easy to work up a different type of stitch, change colour or add a motif. A spike stitch is a good example of a really simple way to add detail to your crochet projects, and doesn't take too much work to incorporate.

Adding spike stitches in the same colour is a great way of adding subtle texture to your work, and using a contrasting colours is perfect for adding a statement to your projects. Put simply, a spike stitch is one that extends down more than a single row. You form it by going into the usual V space, but on rows that you have already worked. It forms a longer version of the stitch.

To really add some extra flavour to your work, you could mix spike stitches with crossed stitches, working in the stitch ahead before coming back into the previous stitch. In this following tutorial we will show you have to do the most simple spike stitches.

Spike stitches
Add a flourish to your work

01 Insert your hook
Work your next stitch as usual, but insert your hook into the space however many rows beneath your current row as you desire. Here we have chosen one row beneath.

02 Draw up a loop
Bring the yarn over your hook, then pull it back through and draw up a loop to the height of your current row so that it looks level.

03 Complete your stitch
Now complete the stitch as usual. Yarn over (yo) and pull it through all loops on the hook.

Different lengths
These spike stitches are worked into different rows in a contrasting colour. Here we have used the following pattern: *spike stitch into stitch 1 row below, double crochet (dc) in next st, spike into stitch 2 rows below, double crochet in next stitch; repeat from * to end.

Crossed stitches

Give your crochet a more detailed and advanced look with a really simple method

Adding detail to your crochet doesn't need to be difficult, feel like a chore or take too long. In fact, adding a varied stitch during your rows can do a lot to make your work look more interesting, and make it look more impressive than a simple flat piece of crochet.

A crossed stitch really isn't too difficult and can be used with great effect to produce a cable-like look to your projects. You can pair them with multiple other stitches to create a pretty effect that you might not have thought possible due to the simplicity of crochet.

There are three different ways in which you can work a crossed stitch. You can either work the second stitch in front or behind the one before it, or you can wrap it around the first stitch. Patterns may not specify which method you should use, but usually it will reference which option to adopt in the instructions. You will generally be able to follow written out, clear instructions.

All crossed stitches are formed by skipping the next stitch, crocheting into the second stitch from your hook and then going back into the stitch that you missed.

> *Take time to identify the stitches and work carefully to make sure your crossed stitches come out well, especially if working several crossed stitches at once to create a cable effect.*

Did you know?
James Buchanan, US president between 1857 and 1861 liked to crochet in his free time.

Cross behind
The first option

01 Skip a stitch
Skip the next stitch from where you have been working, and then locate the stitch you skipped — this is where you will work next.

02 Tilt your stitches
Either tilt your work forward or hold down the previous stitch with your thumb while you insert the hook, working behind the first stitch.

03 Complete the cross
Yarn over (yo) your inserted hook, then complete your stitch as required. That's it!

Cross in front
A similar process

This is a bit tricky

01 Skip the stitch
As with working behind, skip the next stitch from where you have been working, then locate the stitch you skipped. This is where you will work next.

02 Push back
This time, instead of tilting your work forward to work behind it, push it back so you can complete the stitch into the skipped stitch from the front.

03 Complete the stitch
Insert your hook into the skip stitch and then complete the stitch as you would usually.

Wrapped
The third and final option

01 Yarn over
Yarn over and insert your hook into the skipped stitch, working in front of the previous stitch.

02 Yarn to the back
With the yarn at the back of your work, yarn over and draw up a loop, bring the loop around the front of the first stitch.

03 Complete the stitch
Complete the stitch as usual. The second stitch will enclose the base of the first one.

Post stitches

Add texture to your work by using post stitches, which can be worked both in front of and behind the previous row

Post stitches can be used to add texture to your work and, when worked in the correct pattern, they can create a distinctive ribbing effect. You can see the a good stitch pattern to create ribbing using this stitch on page 124 (post stitch rib). Usually post stitches are worked around treble crochets (tr) or bigger stitches, as double crochets (dc) aren't really tall enough to get your hook around. However, they can be done quite easily if that is what you want to do, so just follow this guide. It sees you insert your hook around the stitch rather than into the top V to create your next stitch. You can work by inserting your hook from front to back or from back to front, which creates a different visual depending on which side of the piece of crochet you're looking at.

Front post stitch
Insert your hook from front to back

01 Front to back to front
To work a front post treble crochet you need to yarn over (yo) then insert your hook into the gap between the posts of the row below from front to back, around the post next on the row and come through the other side back to the front of your work.

02 Draw up a loop
Yarn over and draw up a loop by pulling the working yarn back through to the right side of your crochet.

03 Complete your stitch
Now complete you stitch as usual.

Back post stitch
Insert your hook from back to front

Before

After

01 Back to front to back
As the opposite to the front post stitch, you will take your hook to the back of your work, yarn over, and then insert your hook into the gap between posts coming from the back to the front, around the post and out of the back.

02 Yarn over and loop
Yarn over and draw up a loop back to where you started the stitch.

03 Complete your stitch
Now complete your stitch as normal.

Chainless foundations
Create your first row without making a chain first

Creating your foundation chain and the subsequent first row of crochet can sometimes result in the chain becoming twisted, but this can be avoided by starting your project with a chainless foundation instead. This combines the foundation chain and the first row in a initial row of crochet rather than two. Using a chainless foundation is a great way to create a stretchy edging compared to a more rigid chain start. Given that you are working the two rows at once, it does take a little longer to work up the chainless foundation than a foundation chain, but it is easier to work your second row into the chainless foundation than into the chain, as you don't have to worry about your chain becoming too tight or twisting while you work into it.

Foundation double crochet (fdc)
Create your first two rows at once

01 Chain two
To get going, the first step in creating your foundation double crochet (fdc) is to chain two. You will be making your first crochet into the second chain from the hook.

02 Insert your hook
Insert your hook into the second chain your from hook, yarn over (yo) and draw up a loop.

Strong foundation
Chainless foundation stitches form vertically so the chain part of the stitch is at the bottom, on the left, and the tops of the stitches are formed on the right.

03 Create the chain
Now yarn over once more and pull the yarn through the first loop on your hook. This forms the chain stitch that you will create your first double crochet (dc) into.

04 Yarn over
Now yarn over your hook and pull through the two loops that are on your hook. You have now created your first double crochet.

05 Create your next double crochet
Insert your hook under the top and back loops of the chain, yarn over and draw up the loop. Make sure it is level before you continue to work the stitch. If you make it too tight it will be difficult to start your next stitch. Now repeat Steps 03 and 04, repeating until you've made the right number of stitches.

05 Keep going
Each following foundation double crochet is worked into the two loops that form the chain at the bottom of the stitch you have just worked.

Create longer chainless foundation stitches
You don't just have to create your first row with double crochets; you can create longer stitches simply by following the same system. You can create a chainless foundation with half treble (htr) and treble (tr) crochets. You merely have to complete the stitch in the same way as you usually would once you have created the 'chain' that you will be working into.

Linked stitches

Close up the loose-looking stitches with this simple technique

Tall crochet stitches can end up looking quite loose, especially when the gaps between them are quite big. You can fix this by using linked stitches to close up the gaps. It helps create a solid fabric and produces a nice texture across them as well. You can apply linked stitches to anything taller than a double crochet (dc) by replacing the first yarn over(s) (yo) at the start of the stitch with a loop that links it to the previous stitch. It should be noted that you won't be counting the turning chain (t-ch)

when you use this technique. Here we have used a linked treble crochet (ltr). It can be a little fiddly, but once you get the hang of it, like most crochet techniques, it's easy!

> *"It can be a little fiddly, but once you get the hang of it"*

Linked stitches
Close gappy stitches

01 Foundation chain
Make a foundation chain for the number of stitches required in your pattern, then do an extra two chains. Insert your hook into the second chain from the hook, yarn over and draw up a loop. Insert your hook into the next chain, yarn over and draw up a loop. You will have three loops on your hook.

02 Do a treble
Now work the remainder of the stitch as a standard treble (tr) stitch. Yarn over, draw through two loops, yarn over, draw through two loops. You have now completed your first linked stitch. You will notice there is a horizontal bar half way up the stitch, this is where your next stitch will link to.

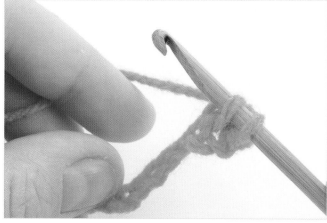

03 Top to bottom
Insert your hook into the horizontal bar from top to bottom.

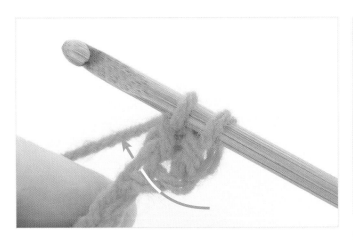

04 Draw up a loop

Yarn over, draw up a loop (this replaces the yarn over at the start of a standard treble crochet). Insert your hook into the next chain.

05 Complete the treble

Now continue with the treble crochet. Yarn over, draw up a loop, (yarn over, and draw through two loops) twice. Repeat from Steps 03 to 05 until the end of the row.

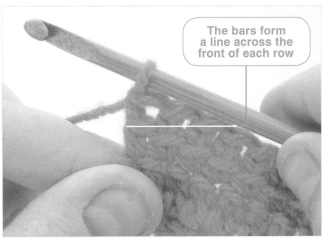

The bars form a line across the front of each row

06 Chain 2

To start a new row, chain two and turn your work. Insert the hook into the second chain from the hook, yarn over and draw up a loop. Insert your hook into the first stitch (at the base of the chain), and repeat Step 05 to complete the linked treble crochet.

07 Carry along the row

For each additional linked treble crochet, draw up a loop from the horizontal bar of the previous linked treble crochet. Insert your hook into the next stitch, as you would any other stitch. Now complete as you have done throughout the rest of the tutorial.

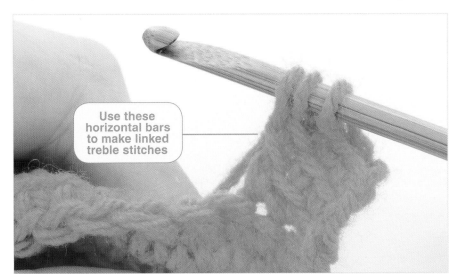

Use these horizontal bars to make linked treble stitches

Link bigger stitches

You can use this technique to link taller stitches. Simply yarn over at the beginning of the stitch with a linked loop, and complete the stitch as usual. To link a double treble stitch (dtr), draw up a loop in the horizontal bar one- and two-thirds down the previous stitch (or the second and third chains of a chain three turning chain) to begin the stitch.

Cluster stitches

Join any number of stitches together to form a cluster

Cluster stitches is a term that can be used to define several different types of collected stitches, but the most basic type are several incomplete stitches that are joined together at the top to form a triangle. Cluster stitches can be used as decreases, can form patterns when used with a combination of other stitches and chains.

There are no strict rules to follow when it comes to the number of stitches you can use in your cluster, and you can use any long sort of stitch. The pattern you are using will specify what combination of stitches should be used for that pattern, and will never simply define it as a cluster. In this tutorial we will teach you how to do a basic four-treble cluster (4-tr) stitch.

> "There are no strict rules to follow when it comes to the number of stitches you can use in your cluster, and you can use any long sort of stitch"

Cluster stitch
Form a four-treble cluster stitch

01 Start your cluster
Yarn over (yo) your hook, insert the tip into the next stitch and draw up a loop.

02 Continue the treble (tr)
Yarn over your hook again and draw the yarn through two loops on the hook. Leave the remaining two loops on the hook!

03 Repeat
Rather than completing the treble crochet, you will yarn over your hook and insert it into the next stitch before drawing up another loop.

04 Keep going
Rather than completing the treble crochet, you will yarn over your hook and insert it into the next stitch before drawing up another loop.

05 Repeat twice more
Now repeat Steps 03 and 04 twice. You will end up with five loops left on your hook and half-completed four stitches.

06 Through the loops
Yarn over and draw the yarn through all five loops on the hook. This completes your cluster.

Not a bobble...
The cluster stitch is not to be confused with the bobble stitch, which is often referred to by the same name but the end result will be altogether different.

Puff stitches

Use puff stitches to create a reversible, cushioned fabric using half treble crochet stitches

Puff stitches are some of the most unusual crochet stitches you will come across. They don't involve the usual method of completing a stitch every two loops. Instead, a puff stitch sees you draw up loops to the height of the other stitches and secure these longer, puffed-out pieces of yarn with a stitch at the top. Puff stitches look identical on either side and work brilliantly for projects such as blankets and coasters, when you want them to work either way up. Puff stitches can take a little while to get used to, but just make sure you work them loosely, and you'll get the hang of it in no time at all.

> *"Puff stitches look identical on either side and work brilliantly for projects such as blankets and coasters"*

Puff stitch
Create a reversible stitch

01 Start the puff stitch
Yarn over (yo) and insert your hook into the next stitch. Draw up a loop. You should have three loops on your hook. Do not pull the working yarn through any of the loops.

02 Draw up
Careful not to pull on the stitch you have worked into, pull the loop up to the desired height. Level it with the height of the other worked stitches. Do not pull too tightly and let the yarn lie quite loosely.

03 Hold the loops

Make sure the loops don't lose their height by keeping the tip of your finger on top of them as you work your next steps.

04 Continue the stitch

Ensuring that you have kept the tension loose, yarn over and insert your hook into the same stitch, yarn over and pull up another loop to the same height. You will have five loops on your hook.

06 Complete the stitch

Yarn over and carefully draw the yarn through all seven loops on the hook, finishing your cluster.

05 Create another loop

Repeat — yarn over, insert your hook, yarn over and draw up a loop to the same height — until have seven unworked loops on your hook.

TOP TIP

When completing the last step, hold gently onto the base of the worked stitches to support the structure as you draw the yarn through the stitches. The more you practise, the easier you will find it to pull through all the stitches with ease.

Popcorn stitches

Add texture to your crochet with the appropriately named popcorn stitch

Popcorn stitches are a great way to add texture to your projects and are one of the only stitches you will use where you need to remove your hook from the working loop in order to complete it. The first time you do this it is quite scary but don't panic, it will produce a fun stitch in the end and it's really easy to do. A popcorn stitch sees you create several treble (tr) crochets into a single stitch and then collect them together at the top with a chain stitch. This is what makes it stand out from the fabric. Worked in a thinner yarn it can add fun details, and in a chunky one it can add dramatic and eye-catching finishes.

01 Treble crochets
Work four treble crochets into the next stitch.

02 Remove your hook
Pull the yarn out a little further than usual, and remove your hook from the current stitch. Be careful not to let it unravel.

03 Insert your hook
Insert your hook from front to back under both loops of the top of the first treble crochet you made at the start of the popcorn stitch.

04 Get the working loop
Instead of pulling your working yarn over your hook as you would usually, insert the hook into the working loop and pull on the working yarn until it is the usual size around the hook.

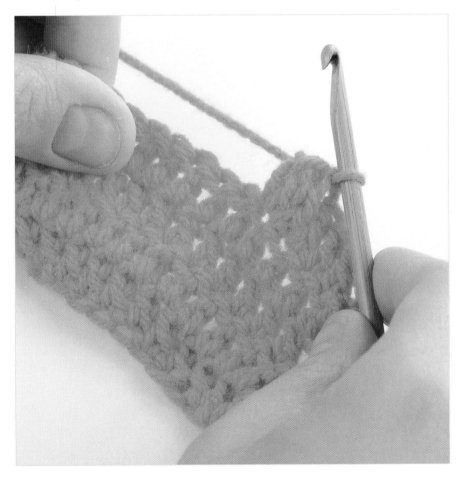

05 Draw it through
Draw the working loop through the top of the first stitch and this will complete the popcorn stitch. Some patterns will dictate that you close the popcorn stitch with a chain stitch. Check the pattern that you are using. If it doesn't mention it, just finish it here.

Motifs

Create motifs as part of a whole project or as a final embellishment

The term 'motif' might be a little confusing, as you may think it will simply refer to the additional little pieces that you add to your crochet projects once complete. In actual fact, when it comes to crochet, a motif is any sort of smaller piece of crochet you create that's intended to be part of a bigger project, whether this is indeed a flower to be added to a hat, or a granny square intended to be sewn together with other types of square to create a larger final project. Squares are the most common type of motif (most families will somewhere have a granny square blanket, we can all but guarantee it...) but they aren't just limited to something your granny made in order to pass down. You can create scarves, tops and even dresses out of the trusty granny square. They're versatile and they are so simple to make.

The best thing about motifs is that they aren't limited to a type of yarn, a weight or thickness of any kind. You can make them out of any yarn you have lying around and even with the scraps you are left with at the end of your other projects. Perfect for making a crazy combination blanket!

Starting a motif

One common feature of motifs is that they are always worked in the round. You can find out more on how to do this on page 68. You work from the middle outwards and never turn your work. No matter what the end product of your motif, it will always start out looking like a circle — but don't worry, this is how it is meant to be.

You start your motif with a ring, either through a magic ring or a small collection of chain stitches linked together. From here, the first round is worked into the centre and then joined to create the first lot of stitches. There are sometimes exceptions to this, as some motifs will have you first work into the front loops, before you go on to continue in a spiral into the back loops, only to create a neat layered effect. In fact, we go into this on page 111 with a double flower.

Even if your motif continues to look a bit round as you work, it will eventually turn into the shape it is supposed to be, so rest assured.

Continuing the project

It isn't uncommon for motifs to be worked in different colours for each round that you do, which is what makes them so perfect for using up the ends of your various yarns. Depending on the effect you wish to achieve, you could alternate colours, you could never use the same colour twice, or you can come up with a combination and order of colours that you can change per square to create a really neat-looking blanket, for instance.

For the cleanest result, turn your work every round and fasten on at different points each round; this will stop any wobbly edge where every fasten on happens, and the joins will be less noticeable if they aren't all in one place! To start each round, fasten on your yarn by drawing up a loop and crocheting over the start of the yarn as you work around the motif. This will make it extra secure, as you don't want it falling apart, and with all the ends that you will end up with connecting different colours, it will take less time to darn in any loose ends if you simply crochet them in instead!

Top motif tips

01 Avoid having to darn

With many motifs you will end up with a lot of starts and ends of yarn. We cannot stress enough how much easier life will be when you come to finish up your project if you crochet over any loose ends as you work. Starting yarns are easy to hide in the new colour, and end yarns will soon disappear if you crochet over those as well. By doing this you not only save yourself a lot of time and effort, but you might not even have to pick up a darning needle if you're meticulous about it.

02 Use the same edging colour

While you can make motifs in various colours, it is much easier to join them together neatly with near-invisible seams if you use the same colour on the final round. This means you can use this colour everywhere when joining your motifs without having to worry about it looking obvious.

03 Go large!

You don't need to stick to small motifs. Whoever said they didn't want a massive granny square? Instead of making them with only four or five rounds, make them larger, and then join them together. You may even find it easier to make bigger projects faster if you aren't having to fiddle each time you join a new colour and get into the groove. If you think your work is starting to skew because of the way the stitches are worked slightly to the right each time, simply flip your work over and this will save it!

04 Ignore rounded corners

It's a simple fact that when you crochet a square, the corner will always look a little rounded, unless you have blocked it. But don't worry, this is completely normal. When you connect the squares together they will form the right shape and you don't even realise they were ever rounded in the first place. If you have created one massive motif then you can block the motif instead to form the corners. Check out how to start blocking on page 76.

> *"For the cleanest result, turn your work every round and fasten on at different points each round; this will stop any wobbly edge"*

Solid squares

Add a bit of variety to our granny square blankets with this super simple solid incarnation

Everybody loves a granny square, but sometimes we want our crochet projects to be more than standard. You can mix up those sorts of projects by adding in the occasional solid square. And it's as easy as its gappy cousin. Instead of stitching trebles (tr) into chain spaces (ch-sp), simply put them into the tops of each stitch, as you would with any other project. It can be easy to lose the first stitch after a chain space beneath the four stitches within it, but don't worry — simply pull the stitches back and it will reveal the space to the right of the post that you need to enter into. Each side should have four more stitches, meaning each round should have 16 more stitches than the last. If you keep count, you won't end up with something resembling a trapezium.

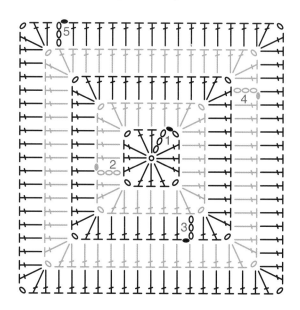

> "It can be easy to lose the first stitch after a chain space beneath the four stitches within it, but don't worry"

TOP TIP It is easy to keep a count of stitches, just remember to add four to the total number on a side each time: 3, 7, 11, 15, 19, 23, 27 and so on.

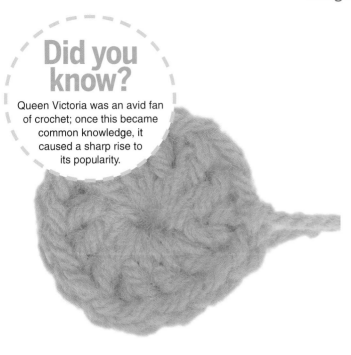

Start your round with a chain start or a magic ring. A magic ring will give a tighter beginning.

Rnd 1: Ch 3 (counts as tr, here and throughout). Working into the ring, 2 tr, ch 1, (3 tr, ch 1) 3 times.
If you are using a magic ring, pull it closed.
Join with a sl st to the top of ch 3 and fasten off.

Rnd 2: Join new yarn to an stitch immediate preceding a ch-sp.
Ch 3, (2 tr, ch 1, 2 tr) in next chain space, *tr in next 3 sts, (2 tr, ch 1, 2 tr) in next ch-sp; repeat from * twice, tr in next 2 sts.
Join with sl st into top of ch 3 and fasten off.

Rnd 3: Join new yarn to an stitch immediate preceding a ch-sp.
Ch 3, (2 tr, ch 1, 2 tr) in next ch-sp, *tr in next 7 sts, (2 tr, ch 1, 2 tr) in next ch-sp; repeat from * twice, tr in next 6 sts.
Join with sl st into top of ch 3 and fasten off.

Every following round: Follow the same pattern, adding an extra 4 sts between ch-sps.

Circle in a square

Start with a circle and end up with a square, this crochet creation is absolutely perfect to stitch together for a granny square motif blanket

The granny square technique doesn't just have to stop at squares. You can use the same technique to create circles and, for an extra flourish in your granny square blanket, you can have circles within squares. You can work them in whatever colour patterns you like, but you can really make the circle detail pop if you use one colour for the circle, followed by another for the square. In the general scheme of working this technique, you will work the first three rounds to form the circle, and then round four works as a transition into the square outline, with the final round working to create the end of the granny square. It might sound a little complicated, but really it's quite simple if you follow these step-by-step directions.

"You can really make the circle detail pop if you use one colour for the circle, and then another for the square"

Circle in a square
Make your granny square more interesting

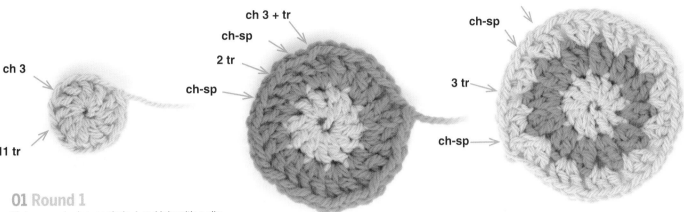

ch 3

11 tr

ch 3 + tr
ch-sp
2 tr
ch-sp

ch 3 + 2 tr
ch-sp
3 tr
ch-sp

01 Round 1
Make a magic ring, or chain 4 and join with a slip stitch (sl st).
  Ch 3 (counts as a tr here and throughout), 11 tr into the ring. Draw your magic ring closed carefully. Join with a sl st into the top of the ch 3 and fasten off.

02 Round 2
Fasten on a new yarn to any stitch. Ch 3, tr in same st, ch 1, (2 tr, ch 1) into next 11 stitches.

03 Round 3
Fasten on with new yarn at any ch-sp. Ch 3, 2 tr in same chain space, ch 1, (3 tr, ch 1) in next 11 ch-sps. Join with a sl st and fasten off.

corner space

edge spaces

04 Round 4
Fasten on with next yarn at any ch-sp. Ch 3, 2 tr in same ch-sp, ch 1, 3 tr in next ch-sp, ch 1, *(3 tr, ch 1, 3 tr, ch 1) in next ch-sp, (3 tr, ch 1) in next 2 ch-sps; repeat from * twice more, (3 tr, ch 1, 3 tr, ch 1) in next ch-sp. Join with sl st to top of ch 3 and fasten off.

05 Round 5
Fasten on at any non-corner ch-sp. Ch 3, 2 tr in same ch-sp, ch 1. Make (3 tr, ch 1) in each edge space, and repeat (3 tr, ch 1) twice in each corner space. Join with a sl st at the top of ch 3 and fasten off.

"Work the first three rounds to form the circle, and then round four works as a transition into the square outline"

Granny squares

Create the most recognisable crochet pattern in the world: the granny square!

Granny square
Make the first square in a project

01 Round 1

Make a magic ring (or chain 4 and join with a sl st into a ring). **Round 1:** Ch 3 (counts as a tr here and throughout). Working into the ring, 2 tr, ch 1, (3 tr, ch 1) 3 times. Pull your magic ring closed gently. Join with a sl st into the stop of the chain 3 and fasten off.

02 Round 2

Fasten on with your next yarn into any ch-sp. Ch 3, (2 tr, ch 1, 3 tr) in chain ch-sp, ch 1, (3 tr, ch 1, 3 tr, ch 1) into next 3 ch-sp. Join with sl st to top of ch 3. Fasten off.

04 All future rounds

For all further rounds, fasten on at any edge ch-sp. Ch 3, 2 tr in same ch-sp, ch 1. Make (3 tr, ch 1) in each edge space, and repeat (3 tr, ch 1) twice in each corner space. Join with a sl st into top of ch 3.

03 Round 3

Fasten on with next yarn at any edge ch-sp. Ch 3, 2 tr in same ch-sp. Cha 1, *(3 tr, ch 1, 3 tr, ch 1) in next corner ch-sp. 3 dc in next edge ch-sp, ch 1. Repeat from * twice more. (3 tr, ch 1, 3 tr, ch 1) in last corner ch-sp. Join with sl st to top of ch 3. Fasten off.

> **TOP TIP**
> Create as many granny squares as you want and join them together with a stitch of your choice (see page 80). It makes a brilliant blanket and it is an absolute classic!

Granny triangles

Drop a corner and add an extra stitch to each cluster to create a triangle

Granny triangle
Make a variant of the granny square

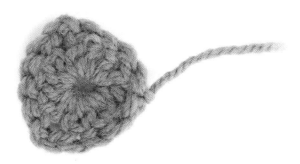

01 Round 1
Make a magic ring (or chain 4 and join with a sl st into a ring).
Round 1: Ch 3 (counts as a tr here and throughout). Working into the ring, 3 tr, ch 2, (4 tr, ch 2) 2 times. Pull your magic ring closed gently. Join with a sl st into the stop of the chain 3 and fasten off.

02 Round 2
Fasten on with your next yarn into any ch-sp. Ch 3, (3 tr, ch 2, 4 tr) in chain ch-sp, ch 1, (4 tr, ch 2, 4 tr, ch 2) into next 3 ch-sp. Join with sl st to top of ch 3. Fasten off.

03 Round 3
Fasten on with next yarn at any edge ch-sp. Ch 3, 3 tr in same ch-sp. Ch 1, *(4 tr, ch 2, 4 tr, ch 2) in next corner ch-sp. 4 tr in next edge ch-sp, ch 1. Repeat from * once more. (4 tr, ch 2, 4 tr, ch 2) in last corner ch-sp. Join with sl st to top of ch 3. Fasten off.

04 All future rounds
For all further rounds:
Fasten on at any edge ch-sp. Ch 3, 3 tr in same ch-sp, ch 2. Make (4 tr, ch 2) in each edge space, and repeat (4 tr, ch 2) twice in each corner space. Join with a sl st into top of ch 3.

Flower motifs

Add embellishments to your projects by creating and attaching separate flowers

Crochet flowers are quick and easy to make. They only take a couple of rounds and a few different stitches to create something that looks more complicated than it actually is. Added to a child's cardigan or to a crocheted hat, these details can really bring a project together. You don't just have to use them as embellishments, however, you could attach a safety pin to the wrong side of the finished flower to use it as a brooch all on its own. Here we have used just one colour but you could easily use multiple hues to give your flowers a boost. You can make flowers with any size yarn, just make sure you have the correct size hook to suit.

Simple flower
Make an easy flower in two rounds

01 Magic ring
Make a magic ring and then chain one.

02 Round one
Double crochet (dc) into your magic ring and then chain two. Repeat this five more times so you end up with six. Pull the ring closed and join it to the first stitch with a slip stitch (sl st).

03 Second round
Into each chain space do the following: slip stitch, chain two, two treble crochets (tr), chain two, slip stitch. Repeat this six times, and your petals will be complete. Fasten off and weave in the ends.

Double flower
Try a more detailed design

01 Start the flower
This flower is worked in a continuous spiral, so don't join the rounds at the end. Start with a magic ring — so six double crochets into it, and then pulling it closed.

02 Round two
Into each stitch from round one do the following: chain two, treble crochet in front loop, chain two, slip stitch in front loop of same stitch.

03 Round three
Fold the petals forwards to expose the back loops. For round three you will work into the back loops of round one. In each of the back loops work the following: chain one, treble crochet. Then slip stitch into the first chain space (ch-sp). You will have made six treble crochets.

04 Final round
Chain two, two treble crochets in the same chain space at the bottom of the chain you just created. Chain two, slip stitch in same chain space. *Chain two, two treble crochets in next chain space, chain two, slip stitch in same chain space. Repeat from * five times. Make six petals. Fasten off and weave in ends.

Fringe
Create a fringe to embellish your scarves or other projects

Adding a fringe at the end of any project can be the final detail you need to make it complete, especially when it comes to scarves. You can customise it in several ways, depending on the colour and the length of the fringe, the number of strands per section that you tie on, and you can also vary the gaps between each knot. If you're using the same colour as your project for your fringe, you can incorporate the ends instead of having to weave them in. And if you're using contrasting colours then you can use it to help secure your weaved-in ends!

It should be easy to figure out how many strands you need for most projects, by counting how many stitches you want to weave your fringe into, knowing how many strands you wish to put into each stitch, and multiplying them together. If you want to avoid doing any maths, you can simply cut some at a time, tie them on and keep going until you're all done!

Fringe technique
Add some detail to your project

01 Round one
Cut a piece of card to the size you require. Make sure that it creates lengths roughly 2cm (1in) longer than the desired fringe length to account for the knots in the yarn.

02 Cut the yarn
Take a sharp pair of scissors to the edge of the card, slip a blade behind the yarn and cut. Each strand will now be the same length!

03 Count up the strands

Decide on how many strands you want on each part of your fringe, remembering that one strand of yarn will create two in the piece of fringe. Fold the strands in half.

04 Pull it through

Using your crochet hook, insert the head through the stitch you wish to add the fringe to. Insert the hook into the middle of the strands.

05 Pull through

Carefully draw the strands through, leaving a loop big enough to slip your fingers into. Alternatively, you can use your hook to pull through the strands.

06 Secure the ends

Once you have pulled all the strands through the loop, be careful not to accidentally pull on one strand more than the others, as this will make the fringe wonky. Pull until the knot is nice and tight. Now repeat until you're finished.

Reverse double crochet

Create a non-stretchy cord edge with the reverse double crochet

Also known as a crab stitch, the reverse double crochet (rdc) is worked in the opposite direction to what you are used to. Admittedly, it can take a little while to get the hang of this, as it completely goes against the natural order of all things crochet. You will start at the left-hand side of the piece and work towards the right. This means that each of the stitches will be twisted so that the usual V formation is hidden and the edge is neatly finished. Note that you can't crochet into a reverse double crochet as it doesn't offer a solid entry point, so make sure you only ever use this technique as a pretty edging to the end of your project.

> "Each of the stitches will be twisted so that the usual V formation is hidden and the edge is neatly finished"

TOP TIP
If you work too quickly your yarn could snag around the last stitch you made and the stitches could tangle together. If this happens, just undo the stitch and start again. Take your time!

Reverse double crochet
Create an elegant bobbled edging

01 Fasten on
Choose any point along the edge of your piece of fabric and chain one. You will work into the previous stitch, the one to the right of your hook, not the one to your left!

02 Start the stitch
Insert your hook as your would usually from front to back.

Work into the same stitch

If you're working all the way around, work your final reverse double crochet into the same stitch as where you fastened on, as this will currently be unworked.

03 Hook facing forward

Yarn over (yo) and draw up a loop, making sure your hook faces towards the left as it would usually. If you twist your hook, you will end up with a mirrored version of a standard double crochet (dc), not a reverse stitch.

04 Complete the stitch

Now complete the stitch as you would a normal double crochet, yarn over and draw through both loops on the hook.

05 Keep going

Continue to work backwards along your edge, making sure not to twist your hook!

06 Reverse around the corner

If you are going around a 90-degree corner, work three reverse double crochets into the same stitch.

Picot edging

Give your work a delicate finish with a picot edging, often used on clothing and lace pieces

Quite simply, picot edging is a collection of chain stitches that can be added to the edge of your crochet project. They are brought together by a double crochet (dc) into the next stitch (or into the bottom of the chain) or by skipping stitches to create larger loops, also know as open picot. It has the benefit of being really simple to do while managing to look incredibly effective. You can make your picot stitches as long or as short as you like, from using only two extra chains to create a small bobble or a whole load of them to create a fun fringe effect.

If you are following a pattern it should state what type of picot edging, and whether to go into the bottom of the chain or into the next stitch (or, of course, how many stitches to skip!).

> "You can make your picot stitches as long or as short as you like, from using only two extra chains to create a small bobble or a whole load of them to create a fun fringe effect"

Picot edging
Add a border to your garments

01 Fasten on
Fasten on your yarn to any stitch, chain one. Double crochet into the first stitch and then chain three.

02 Into the loop
Work into the front loop and left vertical bar of the stitch at the base of your chain.

03 Slip stitch
Complete your picot stitch with a slip stitch (sl st). Insert your hook into the vertical bar of the double crochet below, draw up a loop and draw it through the loop on the hook.

04 Double crochet
Now do a few double crochets along the edge in order to space out the picot edge.

> **TOP TIP**
> It is best to count your stitches before you start and do a little bit of maths to figure out how many picot stitches you want, and how often they will need to occur.

05 Picot again
Now repeat Steps 01 to 03 to create another picot. And repeat.

06 Around the bend
To picot on a corner, continue as your would for a normal double crocheted edge, making three double crochets into the corner stitch. Continue to count your stitches and make sure you keep the gaps between them the same.

Stitch pattern gallery

Armed with only a few simple stitches in your repertoire, there are many pretty and interesting fabrics you can make

With just three basic crochet stitches — double crochet (dc), treble crochet (tr) and half treble crochet (htr) — you can create a really wide variety of patterns, and these can be used to make many different projects. With these easy stitch patterns you could create a dishcloth, a scarf or even a blanket — anything rectangular in shape. These are all items that don't require strict measurements, so would make a great starter project if you're trying to improve your tension and technique.

To start off these patterns, make a foundation chain to your desired length, then keep following the pattern until the piece is as large as you would like it to be.

> *"With these easy stitch patterns, you could create a dishcloth, a scarf or even a blanket — anything rectangular in shape"*

Single crochet ribbing

By crocheting into the back loops (BL) you will create a horizontal ridge that forms into a stretchy ribbed pattern.

Ch any number of sts.

Row 1: dc in 2nd ch from hook and in every remaining ch across.

Row 2: ch 1, turn, dc in BL of each st across.

Rep Row 2 for pattern.

Granite stitch

This simple and pretty stitch is also known as moss or seed stitch.

Ch an even number of sts.

Row 1: dc in 2nd ch from hook and in every remaining ch across.

Row 2: ch 1, turn, *dc in next st, ch 1, sk next st; rep from * across to last st, dc in last st.

Row 3: ch 1, turn, dc in next st, *dc in next ch1-sp, ch 1, sk next st; rep from * across to last 2 sts, dc in next ch1-sp, dc in last st.

Row 4: ch 1, turn, dc in next st, *ch 1, sk next st, dc in next ch1-sp; rep from * across to last 2 sts, ch 1, sk next st, dc in last st.

Rep Rows 3 and 4 for pattern.

Chain mesh

Open and lacy patterns like this are easy to make with a combination of double crochets and chains. It is important to block work like this to really define the pattern.

Ch a multiple of 4 sts plus 2.

Row 1: dc in 2nd ch from hook *ch 5, sk next 3 st, dc in next ch; rep from * across.

Row 2: ch 5 (counts as tr +ch 2), turn, *dc in next ch5-sp, ch 5; rep from * across to end, dc in last stitch.

Row 3: ch 1, turn, dc in next st, ch 5, *dc in next ch5-sp, ch 5; rep from * across to end, dc in 3rd ch of t-ch.

Rep rows 3 and 4 for pattern.

To make a straight edge along the top, follow a Row 3 with Row 4.

Row 4 (optional): ch 4 (counts as htr + ch 2), turn, *dc in next ch5-sp, ch 3; rep from * across to last ch5-sp, dc in last ch5-sp, ch 2, htr in last st.

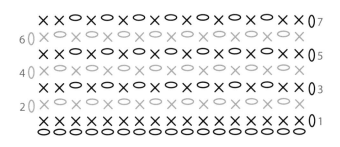

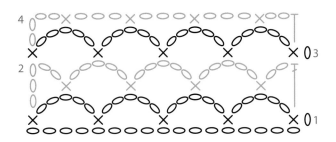

Up-and-down stitch

Using a combination of tall and short stitches produces this lightly textured fabric.

Ch a multiple of 2 sts plus 1.

Row 1: dc in 2nd ch from hook, *tr in next ch, dc in next ch; rep from * across to last ch, tr in last st.

Row 2: ch 1, turn, *dc in next tr, tr in next dc; rep from * across to end.

Rep Row 2 for pattern.

Filet squares

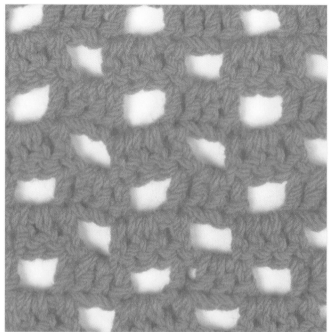

The alternating empty and filled block of stitches are characteristic of filet crochet designs, and can be modified quite simply by adding or subtracting the number of chs and trs for a different look.

Ch a multiple of 6 sts plus 3.

Row 1: tr in 4th ch from hook (unworked chs count as tr), tr in next 2 chs, ch 2, sk next 2 chs, *tr in next 4 chs, ch 2, sk next 2 chs; rep from * across to last ch, tr in last ch.

Row 2: ch 3 (counts as a tr), turn, 2 tr in next ch2-sp, tr in next st, ch 2, sk next 2 sts, *tr in next st, 2 tr in next ch2-sp, tr in next st, ch 2, sk next 2 sts; rep from * across to last st, tr in top of t-ch.

Rep Row 2 for pattern.

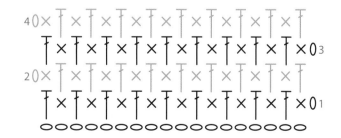

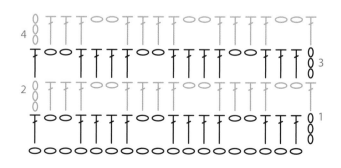

Ripple

This fun rippling wave effect is created simply by stacking increases and decreases.

Ch a multiple of 12 sts plus 3.

Row 1: tr in 4th ch from hook (unworked chs count as tr), tr in next 3 chs, tr2tog twice, *tr in next 3 chs, 2 tr in next 2 chs, tr in next 3 chs, tr2tog twice; rep from * across to last 4 chs, tr in next 3 chs, 2 tr in last ch.

Row 2: ch 3 (counts as tr), turn, tr in same st, tr in next 3 sts, tr2tog twice, *tr in next 3 sts, 2 tr in next 2 sts, tr in next 3 sts, tr2tog twice; rep from * across to last 4 sts, tr in next 3 sts, 2 tr in top of t-ch.

Rep Row 2 for pattern.

Grit stitch

The grit stitch creates a dense and warm pattern, which is perfect for scarves.

Ch a multiple of 2 sts plus 1.

Row 1: dc in 2nd ch from hook and in every remaining ch across.

Row 2: ch 2, turn, sk first st, *(dc,tr) in next st, sk next st; rep from * across to last st, dc in last st.

Row 3: ch 2, turn, (dc, tr) in every dc across, dc in top of t-ch.

Rep Row 3 for pattern.

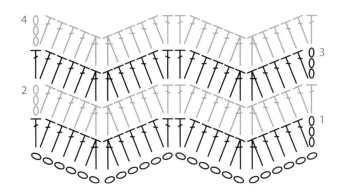

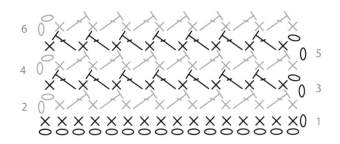

Braided cable stitch

By using crossed and post stitches you can create a 3D cabled effect that you may assume was limited to knitting patterns.

Chain a multiple of 20.

Row 1: dc in 2nd ch from the hook. dc to end of row.

Row 2: ch 3, turn, tr in each st.

Row 3: ch 1, turn, dc in each st.

Row 4: ch 3, turn, tr into the same st and the 2 next sts, *FPdt into next st from tr round, Skip 1, FPdt, FPdt, go back & FPdt into the skipped stitch, FPtc into next st from dc round, dc into next 3 sts* Repeat to end

Row 5: ch 1, turn, dc in each stitch.

Note: From here on out all FPdt's will be made into the FPdt's previous rows.

Diamond fans

Special stitch

V st: (tr, ch 1, tr) in specified st.

Ch a multiple of 4 sts plus 2.

Row 1: dc in 2nd ch from hook, *ch 5, sk next 3 chs, dc in next ch; rep from * across to end.

Row 2: ch 3 (counts as tr), turn, tr in same st, ch 1, *dc in next ch5-sp, ch 1, V st in next dc, ch 1; rep from * across to last ch5-sp, dc in last ch5-sp, ch 1, 2 tr in last dc.

Row 3: ch 1, turn, dc in next st, ch 5, *dc in top of V st, ch 5; rep from * across to end, dc in top of t-ch.

Rep Rows 2 and 3 for pattern.

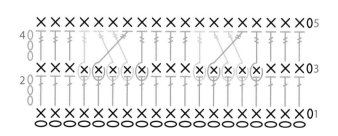

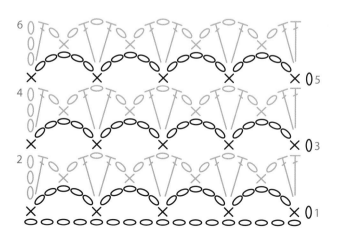

Popcorn squares

Special stitch

Popcorn: make 4 tr in specified st.
Remove hook from working loop, insert hook from front
to back in top of 1st tr made, reinsert hook into working loop, and
draw through both loops on hook.

Ch a multiple of 4 sts.
Row 1: dc in 2nd ch from hook, *ch 1, sk next ch, dc in next ch; rep
from * across to end.
Row 2: ch 3 (counts as tr), turn, tr in next ch1-sp, *ch 1, popcorn
in next ch1-sp, ch 1, tr in next ch1-sp; rep from * across to last st, tr
in last st.
Row 3: ch 1, turn, dc in next st, ch 1, *dc in next ch1-sp, ch 1; rep
from * across to last 2 sts, sk next st, dc in last st.
Rep Rows 2 and 3 for pattern.

V bobbles

Special stitch

Bobble: (yo, insert hook into st and draw up a loop, yo and draw
through 2 loops on hook) twice, yo and draw vthrough all 3 loops
on hook.
V bobble: (bobble, ch 1, bobble) in specified st.

Ch a multiple of 4 sts plus 3.
Row 1: V bobble in 5th ch from hook (unworked chains count as
tr), sk next ch, *tr in next ch, sk next ch, V bobble in next ch, sk
next ch; rep from * across to last ch, tr in last ch.
Row 2: ch 3 (counts as tr), turn, V bobble in top of next V bobble,
*tr in next tr, V bobble in top of next V bobble; rep from * across
to last st, tr in top of t-ch.
Rep Row 2 for pattern.

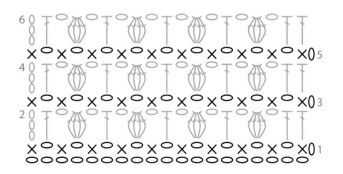

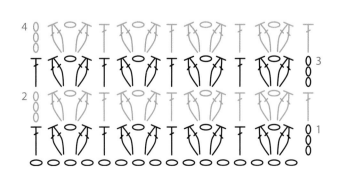

Post stitch rib

Ch a multiple of 2 sts.

Row 1: tr in 4th ch from hook (unworked chains count as tr), tr in each remaining ch across.

Row 2: ch 3 (counts as tr), turn, *FPtr in next st, BPtr in next st; rep from * across to last st, tr in top of t-ch.

Rep Row 2 for pattern.

Waffle stitch

Ch a multiple of 3 sts plus 2.

Row 1: tr in 4th ch from hook (unworked chains count as tr), tr in each remaining ch across.

Row 2: ch 3 (counts as tr, here and throughout), turn, *FPtr in next st, tr in next 2 sts; rep from * across to last 2 sts, FPtr in next st, tr in top of t-ch.

Row 3: ch 3, turn, *tr in next st, FPtr in next 2 sts; rep from * across to last 2 sts, tr in next st, tr in top of t-ch.

Rep Rows 2 and 3 for pattern.

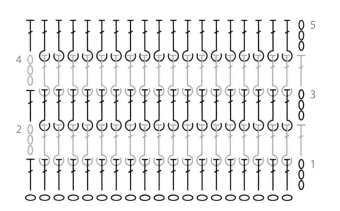

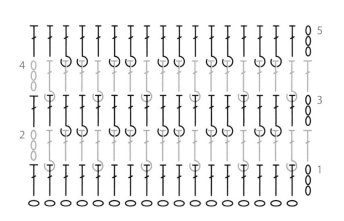

Basket weave

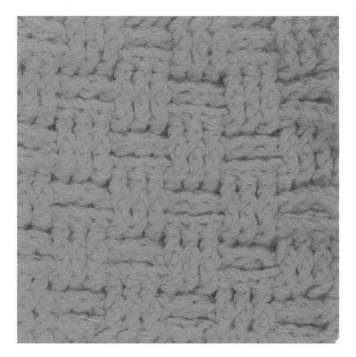

Ch a multiple of 6 sts plus 4.
Row 1: tr in 4th ch from hook (unworked chains count as tr), tr in each remaining ch across.
Row 2: ch 3 (counts as tr, here and throughout), turn, *FPtr in next 3 sts, BPtr in next 3 sts; rep from * across to last st, tr in top of t-ch.
Row 3: rep Row 2.
Row 4: ch 3, turn, *BPtr in next 3 sts, FPtr in next 3 sts; rep from * across to last st, tr in top of t-ch.
Row 5: rep Row 4.
  Rep Rows 2 through 5 for pattern.

Diamond overlay

Ch a multiple of 6 sts plus 3.
Row 1: dc in 2nd ch from hook and in each remaining ch across.
Row 2: ch 3 (counts as tr, here and throughout), turn, *sk next 2 sts, dtr in next st, tr in 2 skipped sts (working behind st just made), sk next st, tr in next 2 sts, dtr in skipped st (working in front of sts just made); rep from * across to last st, tr in last st.
Row 3: ch 1, turn, dc in each st across.
Row 4: ch 3, turn, *sk next st, tr in next 2 sts, dtr in skipped st (working in front of sts just made), sk next 2 sts, dtr in next st, tr in 2 skipped sts (working behind st just made); rep from * across to last st, tr in last st.
Row 5: rep Row 3.
  Rep Rows 2 through 5 for pattern.

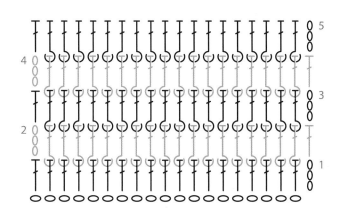

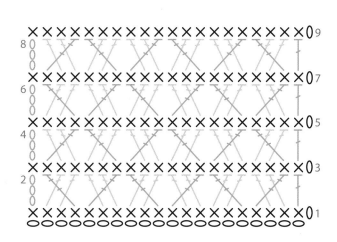

Triangle spaces

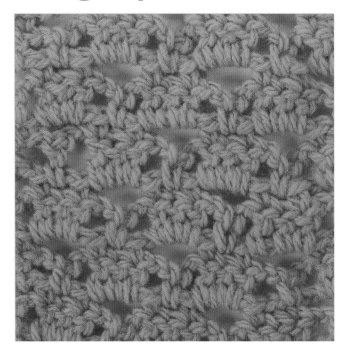

Ch a multiple of 6 sts plus 2.
Row 1: dc in 2nd ch from hook, dc in next ch, ch 3, sk next 3 chs, dc in next ch, *ch 1, sk next ch, dc in next ch, ch 3, sk next 3 chs, dc in next ch; rep from * across to last ch, dc in last ch.
Row 2: ch 1, turn, dc in next st, ch 2, 3 tr in next ch3-sp, *ch 2, dc in next ch1-sp, ch 2, 3 tr in next ch3-sp; rep from * across to last 2 sts, ch 2, sk next st, dc in last st.
Row 3: ch 4 (counts as tr + ch 1), turn, dc in next tr, ch 1, sk next tr, dc in next tr, *ch 3, dc in next tr, ch 1, sk next tr, dc in next tr; rep from * across to end, ch 1, tr in last dc.
Row 4: ch 3 (counts as tr), turn, tr in next ch1-sp, ch 2, dc in next ch1-sp, *ch 2, 3 tr in next ch3-sp, ch 2, dc in next ch1-sp; rep from * across to last space, ch 2, 2 tr in t-ch space.
Row 5: ch 1, turn, dc in next 2 trs, ch 3, *dc in next tr, ch 1, sk next tr, dc in next tr, ch 3; rep from * across to last 2 sts, dc in next tr, dc in top of t-ch.
  Rep Rows 2 through 5 for pattern.

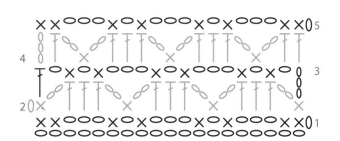

Tumbling blocks

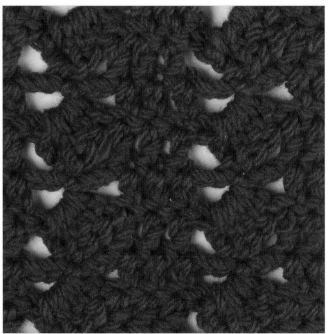

Special stitch
To work a stitch around the post of a previous stitch, insert the hook under the stitch, instead of into it, and crochet around it.

  Ch a multiple of 8 sts plus 5.
Row 1: tr in 4th ch from hook (unworked chs count as tr), *tr in next ch, sk next 2 chs, tr in next ch, ch 3, 3 tr around post of tr just worked, sk next 2 chs, tr in next 2 chs; rep from * across to last ch, tr in last ch.
Row 2: ch 3 (counts as tr, here and throughout), turn, *tr in next 2 trs, ch 2, dc in ch3-sp, ch 2, sk next tr, tr in next tr; rep from * across to last 2 sts, tr in next tr, tr in top of t-ch.
Row 3: ch 3, turn, *tr in next 2 trs, tr in next dc, ch 3, 3 tr around post of tr just worked, tr in next tr; rep from * across to last 2 sts, tr in next tr, tr in top of t-ch.
  Rep Rows 2 and 3 for pattern.

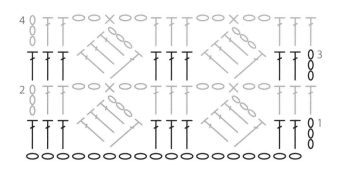

Mini picot mesh

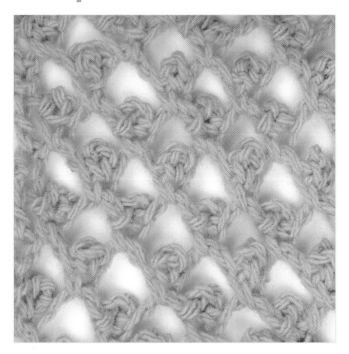

Special stitch

 Picot: ch 3, sl st into front loop and left vertical bar of dc at base of ch.

Ch a multiple of 3 sts plus 2.
Row 1: dc in 2nd ch from hook, *ch 3, sk next 2 chs, dc in next ch, picot; rep from * across to last 3 chs, ch 3, sk next 2 chs, dc in last ch.
Row 2: ch 4 (counts as tr + ch 1), turn, *dc in next ch3-sp, picot, ch 3; rep from * across to last ch3-sp, dc in last ch3-sp, picot, ch 1, tr in last st.
Row 3: ch 1, turn, dc in next st, ch 3, *dc in next ch3-sp, picot, ch 3; rep from * across to end, dc in 3rd ch of t-ch.
Rep Rows 2 and 3 for pattern.
You can omit the picots from the final row to give a straighter top edge. And with lacy patterns like this, blocking is essential to open the mesh and really show off the stitch pattern.

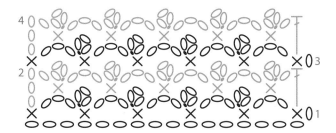

Offset arches

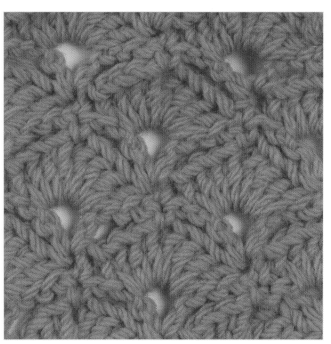

Special stitch

 Shell: (4 tr, ch 1, 4 tr) in specified st.

 V st: (tr, ch 1, tr) in specified st.in specified st.

Ch a multiple of 8 sts plus 2.
Row 1: dc in 2nd ch from hook, *sk next 3 chs, shell in next ch, sk next 3 chs, dc in next ch; rep from * across to end.
Row 2: ch 3 (counts as tr, here and throughout), turn, tr in same st, ch 2, *dc in top of next shell, ch 2, V st in next dc, ch 2; rep from * across to last shell, dc in top of last shell, ch 2, 2 tr in last dc.
Row 3: ch 3, turn, 4 tr in same st, *dc in next dc, shell in top of next V st; rep from * across to last dc, dc in next dc, 5 tr in top of t-ch.
Row 4: ch 1, turn, dc in next st, ch 2, *V st in next dc, ch 2, dc in top of next shell, ch 2; rep from * across to last dc, V st in last dc, ch 2, dc in top of t-ch.
Row 5: ch 1, turn, dc in next st, *shell in top of next V st, dc in next dc; rep from * across to end.
Rep Rows 2 through 5 for pattern.

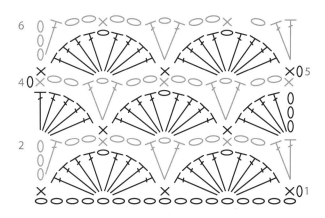

Starter projects
Practise your skills with these projects

130 Squares baby blanket
★★★☆☆

134 Teddy bear
★★☆☆☆

136 T-rex
★★★☆☆

138 Textured hot water bottle cosy
★★★★★

140 Aran cushion cover
★★★★☆

144 Traditional tea cosy
★★★☆☆

146 Spring flower brooch
★★☆☆☆

148 Lace shell-edged shawl
★★★☆☆

152 Cosy alpaca mittens
★★☆☆☆

154 Honeycomb belle hat
★★★☆☆

156 Jumbo rib scarf
★★☆☆☆

Star ratings
These star ratings indicate difficulty level, so pick a pattern based on your ability.

Squares baby blanket

Practise making squares, changing colours and crocheting in the round to make this adorable blanket

Difficulty ★★★☆☆

Skills needed

Joining new yarn
Changing colours
Chain start
Blocking
Joining
Solid squares
Circle in a square
Granny squares
Reverse single crochet

Finished measurements

Blanket measures 80cm (31½in) x 80cm (31½in)

Hook

4mm (US G/6) crochet hook

Yarn

Sublime Baby Cashmere Merino Silk DK
Fibre content: 75% extra fine merino, 20% silk,
5% cashmere
Ball measurements: 50g/116m/126yd
Total meterage/yardage for project:
approx 1624m/1764yd
MC (main colour): Pebble, 006; 8 balls
CC (contrast colours):
Colour 1: Vanilla, 003; 2 balls
Colour 2: Bounty blue, 493; 2 balls
Colour 3: Little Lobby, 494; 2 balls
Colour 4: Pip, 381; 2 balls

Tension (Gauge)

One square to measure 12 x 12cm (4¾ x 4¾in) using 4mm (US G/6) crochet hook, or size required to obtain correct tension.

Notions

Tapestry needle

Pattern notes

Weaving in the ends as you complete each square will make piecing your blanket together much quicker.

Blocking makes a huge difference to the finish and handle of the blanket, and is well worth the effort.

There are 12 colour combinations for each square: Rounds 1, 5, 6 and 7 are always worked with MC.

For the feature rounds use the following combinations:

	CC1	CC2
1:	Colour 1	Colour 2
2:	Colour 1	Colour 3
3:	Colour 1	Colour 4
4:	Colour 2	Colour 1
5:	Colour 2	Colour 3
6:	Colour 2	Colour 4
7:	Colour 3	Colour 1
8:	Colour 3	Colour 2
9:	Colour 3	Colour 4
10:	Colour 4	Colour 1
11:	Colour 4	Colour 2
12:	Colour 4	Colour 3

Pattern

SQUARE 1 — GRANNY IN THE MIDDLE

(Make 12 squares — 1 in each of the 12 colour combinations)
Using MC, make 4 ch and join with sl st to form a ring.
Round 1 (MC): ch 3 (counts as 1 tr), 2 tr into ring, ch 2, (3 tr into ring, ch 2) 3 times, join with sl st in third ch of ch 3, fasten off.
Round 2 (CC1): Join CC1 in any corner ch 2 sp. ch 3 (counts as 1 tr), (2 tr, ch 2, 3 tr) into same ch 2 sp, *ch 1, (3 tr, ch 2, 3 tr) into next ch 2 sp; rep from * twice more, ch 1, join with sl st in third ch of ch 3, fasten off.
Round 3 (CC2): Join CC2 in any corner ch 2 sp. ch 3 (counts as 1 tr), (2 tr, ch 2, 3 tr) into same ch 2 sp,
*ch 1, 3 tr into next ch 1 sp, ch 1, (3 tr, ch 2, 3 tr) into next corner ch 2 sp; rep from * twice more, 3 tr into next edge ch sp, ch 1, join with sl st in third ch of ch 3, do not fasten off.
Round 4 (CC2): sl st into each of next 2 tr and into next corner ch 2 sp. ch 3 (counts as 1 tr), (2 tr, ch 2, 3 tr) into same ch 2 sp, *(ch 1, 3 tr into next ch 1 sp) twice, ch 1, (3 tr, ch 2, 3 tr) into next corner ch 2 sp; rep from * twice more, (ch 1, 3 tr into next ch 1 sp) twice, ch 1, join with sl st in third ch of ch 3, fasten off.
Round 5 (MC): Join MC in any corner ch 2 sp. ch 3 (counts as 1 tr), (1 tr, ch 2, 2 tr) into same ch 2 sp, *(1 tr into each of next 3 tr, 1 tr into next ch 1 sp) 3 times, 1 tr into each of next 3 tr, (2 tr, ch 2, 2 tr) into corner ch 2 sp; rep from * twice more, (1 tr into each of next 3 tr, 1 tr into next ch 1 sp) 3 times, 1 tr into each of next 3 tr, join with sl st into third ch of ch 3, do not fasten off.
Round 6 (MC): ch 1 (does not count as st), 1 dc into each tr of prev round, working 5 dc into each corner ch 2 sp, join with sl st into first dc, do not fasten off.
Round 7 (MC): ch 1 (does not count as st), 1 dc into each dc of prev round, working 3 dc into centre of 5 dc corner group, join with sl st into first dc.
Fasten off.

SQUARE 2 — CIRCLE IN A SQUARE

(Make 12 squares — 1 in each of the 12 colour combinations)
Using MC, work 4 ch and join with sl st to form a ring.
Round 1 (MC): ch 3 (counts as 1 tr), 15 tr into ring, join with sl st into third ch of ch 3, fasten off.

Donna Jones

Donna Jones designs, edits, writes and teaches handknit and crochet. First taught to knit by her mother when she was four years old, she has been surrounded by yarn for as long as she can remember. She firmly believes creative expression is essential for our wellbeing and aims to facilitate this in others. To find more about Donna, visit her website at donnajonesdesigns.co.uk or find her on Instagram @djonesdesigns.

ALSO BY DONNA:
Aran cushion cover (p140)
Lace shell-edged shawl (p148)
Jumbo rib scarf (p156)

"You can make more squares to make a bigger blanket, perhaps large enough to cover a double bed"

Round 2 (CC1): Join CC1 in sp between any 2 tr. ch 3 (counts as 1 tr), 1 tr into same sp, 2 tr into sp between each rem tr of prev round, join with sl st into third ch of ch 3.

Round 3 (CC2): Change to CC2. ch 3 (counts as 1 tr), 1 tr into same place, 1 tr into next tr, (2 tr into next tr, 1 tr into next tr) 15 times, join with sl st into third ch of ch 3, do not fasten off.

Round 4 (CC2): ch 4 (counts as 1 dtr), (2 tr, ch 2, 2 tr, 1 dtr) into same tr, *miss 1 tr, 1 htr into each of next 3 tr, 1 dc into each of next 3 tr, 1 htr into each of next 3 tr, miss next tr, (1 dtr, 2 tr, ch 2, 2 tr, 1 dtr) into next tr; rep from * twice more, miss 1 tr, 1 htr into each of next 3 tr, 1 dc into each of next 3 tr, 1 htr into each of next 3 tr, miss next tr, join with sl st into fourth ch of ch 4, fasten off.

Round 5 (MC): Join MC into any corner ch 2 sp. ch 3 (counts as 1 tr), (1 tr, ch 2, 2 tr) into same sp, *1 tr into each of next 15 sts, (2 tr, ch 2, 2 tr) into corner ch 2 sp; rep from * twice more, 1 tr into each of next 15 sts, join with sl st into third ch of ch 3, do not fasten off.

Round 6 (MC): ch 1 (does not count as st), 1 dc into each tr of prev round, working 5 dc into each corner ch 2 sp, join with sl st into first dc.

Round 7 (MC): ch 1 (does not count as st), 1 dc into each dc of prev round, working 3 dc into centre of 5 dc corner group, join with sl st into first dc.
Fasten off.

SQUARE 3 — SOLID SQUARE

(Make 12 squares — 1 in each of the 12 colour combinations)
Using MC, work 4 ch and join with sl st to form a ring.

Round 1 (MC): ch 3 (counts as 1 tr), 2 tr into ring, ch 2, (3 tr into ring, ch 2) 3 times, join with sl st into third ch of ch 3, fasten off.

Round 2 (CC1): Join CC1 in any corner ch 2 sp. ch 3 (counts as 1 tr), (1 tr, ch 2, 2 tr) into same ch 2 sp, *1 tr into each of next 3 tr, (2 tr, ch 2, 2 tr) into next ch 2 sp; rep from * twice more, 1 tr into each of next 3 tr, join with sl st into third ch of ch 3, do not fasten off.

Round 3 (CC1): Sl st into next tr and into next corner ch 2 sp, ch 3 (counts as 1 tr), (1 tr, ch 2, 2 tr) into same ch 2 sp, *1 tr into each of next 7 tr, (2 tr, ch 2, 2 tr) into next ch 2 sp; rep from

* twice more, 1 tr into each of next 7 tr, join with sl st into third ch of ch 3, fasten off.

Round 4 (CC2): Join CC2 in any corner ch 2 sp, ch 3 (counts as 1 tr), (1 tr, ch 2, 2 tr) into same ch 2 sp, *1 tr into each of next 11 tr, (2 tr, ch 2, 2 tr) into next ch 2 sp; rep from * twice more, 1 tr into each of next 11 tr, join with sl st into third ch of ch 3, fasten off.

Round 5 (MC): Join MC in any corner ch 2 sp, ch 3 (counts as 1 tr), (1 tr, ch 2, 2 tr) into same ch 2 sp, *1 tr into each of next 15 tr, (2 tr, ch 2, 2 tr) into next ch 2 sp; rep from * twice more, 1 tr into each of next 15 tr, join with sl st into third ch of ch 3, fasten off.

Round 6 (MC): ch 1 (does not count as st), 1 dc into each tr of prev round, working 5 dc into each corner ch 2 sp, join with sl st into first dc.

Round 7 (MC): ch 1 (does not count as st), 1 dc into each dc of prev round, working 3 dc into centre of 5 dc corner group, join with sl st into first dc.
Fasten off.

MAKING UP

Weave in all loose ends. Place the squares in 6 rows of 6 squares each, moving the order about until you are pleased with the layout. Make a note of this layout on paper or take a photograph, so that you can refer to this as you assemble the blanket. Using MC and the flat slip-stitched seam technique (see tutorial on page 83), join the squares into strips of 6 squares, then join these 6 strips together to form the blanket.

BORDER

With RS facing, join MC in any edge dc.
Round 1: ch 1 (does not count as st), 1 dc into each dc around edge, working 3 dc into centre st of 3 dc at each corner, join with sl st into first dc.

Rounds 2-3: Rep Round 1 twice more.
Round 4: Crab stitch edging (reverse double crochet — see tutorial on pages 114-115) - ch 1 (does not count as st), 1 rev dc into each dc around edge, working 3 rev dc into each corner, join with sl st into first rev dc.
Fasten off.

Finishing

Weave in all remaining ends and block the blanket by pinning it out flat, taking care not to stretch it. Spray with cool water to moisten, patting the water into the crochet and leave to dry completely before unpinning.

Teddy bear

Create a sweet companion in the form of a teddy bear with this quick and easy project that would make a perfect baby gift

AMY KEMBER

Amy is a technical writer living in Ottawa, Canada. Her interest in crochet began when she discovered an amigurumi book in a used bookstore. After making a pig, she was instantly hooked. Since 2010, Amy has been designing and selling her own amigurumi patterns on Etsy.www.etsy.com/shop/AmysGurumis/

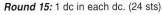

Difficulty ★★☆☆☆

Skills needed

Magic Ring
Joining
Working in the round
Standard decreases

Finished measurements

23 cm tall

Hook

3.75 mm (US F/5)

Yarn

In this project we have used Bernat Handicrafter Cotton.
You will need to use DK weight yarn the follow colours:
Colour: Skin (1 ball)

Notions

1 pair 6 mm safety eyes
Yarn needle
Fibrefill
Brown yarn

Pattern

HEAD

(Using 3.75 mm hook, make a magic ring.
Round 1: 6 dc into ring and pull it closed. (6 sts)
Round 2: 2 dc in each dc. (12 sts)
Round 3: (1 dc in next dc, 2 dc in next dc) 6 times. (18 sts)
Round 4: 1 dc in each dc. (18 sts)
Round 5: (1 dc in each of next 2 dc, 2 dc in next dc) 6 times. (24 sts)
Round 6: (1 dc in each of next 3 dc, 2 dc in next dc) 6 times. (30 sts)
Round 7: (1 dc in each of next 4 dc, 2 dc in next dc) 6 times. (36 sts)

Rounds 8-11: 1 dc in each dc. (4 rnds of 36 sts)
Round 12: (1 dc in each of next 4 dc, dc2tog in next 2 dc) 6 times. (30 sts)
Round 13: (1 dc in each of next 3 dc, dc2tog in next 2 dc) 6 times. (24 sts)
Round 14: (1 dc in each of next 2 dc, dc2tog in next 2 dc) 6 times. (18 sts)

ASSEMBLE THE FACE

Insert 6 mm safety eyes between rnd 1 and rnd 2 of the head and position them 4 sts apart from each other. Embroider a nose and mouth between the eyes on the magic loop and rnd 1 using a yarn needle and
brown yarn. Stuff the head firmly.

Round 15: (1 dc in next dc, dc2tog in next 2 dc) 6 times. (12 sts)
Round 16: (dc2tog in next 2 dc) 6 times. (6 sts)
Round 17: (dc2tog in next 2 dc) 3 times. (3 sts)
Hook yarn and pull through these 3 sts to close.
Fasten off.

BODY

Make a magic ring.
Round 1: Work 6 dc into ring and pull it closed. (6 sts)
Round 2: 2 dc in each dc. (12 sts)
Round 3: (1 dc in next dc, 2 dc in next dc) 6 times. (18 sts)
Round 4: (1 dc in each of next 2 dc, 2 dc in next dc) 6 times. (24 sts)
Round 5: (1 dc in each of next 3 dc, 2 dc in next dc) 6 times. (30 sts)
Rounds 6-13: 1 dc in each dc. (8 rnds of 30 sts)
Round 14: (1 dc in each of next 3 dc, dc2tog in next 2 dc) 6 times. (24 sts)

Round 15: 1 dc in each dc. (24 sts)
Round 16: (1 dc in each of next 2 dc, dc2tog in next 2 dc) 6 times. (18 sts)
Fasten off.

EARS (MAKE 2)

Make a magic ring.
Round 1: 6 dc into ring and pull it closed. (6 sts)
Rounds 2-3: 1 dc in each dc (2 rnds of 6 sts)
Fasten off.

ARMS (MAKE 2)

Make a magic ring.
Round 1: 5 dc into ring and pull it closed. (5 sts)
Round 2: 2 dc in each dc. (10 sts)
Round 3-12: 1 dc in each dc. (10 rnds of 10 sts)
Fasten off.

LEGS (MAKE 2)

Make a magic ring.
Round 1: 8 dc into ring and pull it closed. (8 sts)
Round 2: 2 dc in each dc. (16 sts)
Round 3: 1 dc in each dc. (16 sts)
Round 4: 1 tr in each of next 6 dc, 1 dc in each of next 10 dc. (16 sts)
Round 5: (dc2tog in next 2 tr) 3 times, 1 dc in each of next 10 dc. (13 sts)
Rounds 6-13: 1 dc in each dc. (8 rnds of 13 sts)
Fasten off.

Finishing

Stuff the body, arms and legs. Sew the body to the head. Sew the arms to the body between rnd 15 and rnd 16 and position them 6 sts apart in the front.
Sew the legs flat to the bottom of the body between rnd 2 and rnd 4, and position them close together in the front.

T-rex

Step back into the Jurassic era with this adorable little dinosaur —
it's the perfect playmate for children

MEVLINN GUSICK

Mevlinn is a college graduate with a BFA in Fine Arts Panting. Her
interest in knitting and crochet began when her aunt suggested she
try knitting. It peaked her curiosity and here she is today, crocheting
amigurumi whenever she gets the chance, and giving them to those
she loves.

Difficulty ★ ★ ★ ☆ ☆

Skills needed

Magic Ring
Joining
Back loops only
Working in the round
Standard increases/decreases

Finished measurements

25cm head to tail

Hook

2.75 mm (US C/2)

Yarn

In this pattern we have used Rosario 4 Catitano. You will need an aran weight yarn in the following colours:
Colour 1: Orange (1 ball)
Colour 2: Light yellow (oddments)

Notions

Fibrefill stuffing
12 mm black safety eyes
Scissors
Yarn needle
Stitch marker (optional)

Pattern

BODY

Using col 1, make a magic ring.
Round 1: 6 dc in magic ring. (6 sts)
Round 2: 2 dc in each st around. (12 sts)
Round 3: (2 dc in next st, 1 dc in next st) 6 times. (18 sts)
Round 4: (2 dc in next st, 1 dc in next 2 sts) 6 times. (24 sts)
Round 5: (2 dc in next st, 1 dc in next 3 sts) 6 times. (30 sts)
Round 6: (2 dc in next st, 1 dc in next 4 sts) 6 times. (36 sts)
Round 7: 1 dc in each st around. (36 sts)
Round 8: (2 dc in next st, 1 dc in next 5 sts) 6 times. (42 sts)
Rounds 9-10: 1 dc in each st around. (2 rnds of 42 sts)
Round 11: dc2tog, 1 dc in each remaining st to end. (41 sts)
Rounds 12-14: As rnd 11. (38 sts after rnd 14)
Stuff with toy filling and continue stuffing as you go.
Round 15: dc2tog, 1 dc in next 33 sts, dc2tog, 1 dc in last st. (36 sts)
Round 16: dc2tog, 1 dc in next 31 sts, dc2tog, 1 dc in last st. (34 sts)
Round 17: dc2tog, 1 dc in next 29 sts, dc2tog, 1 dc in last st. (32 sts)
Round 18: dc2tog, 1 dc in next 27 sts, dc2tog, 1 dc in last st. (30 sts)

Round 19: dc2tog, 1 dc in next 25 sts, dc2tog, 1 dc in last st. (28 sts)
Round 20: dc2tog, 1 dc in next 23 sts, dc2tog, 1 dc in last st. (26 sts)
Round 21: dc2tog, 1 dc in each remaining st to end. (25 sts)
Rounds 22-26: As rnd 21. (20 sts after rnd 26)
Fasten off, leaving a long tail for sewing.

HEAD

Using col 1, make a magic ring.
Round 1: 6 dc in magic ring. (6 sts)
Round 2: 2 dc in each st around. (12 sts)
Round 3: (2 dc in next st, 1 dc in next st) 6 times. (18 sts)
Round 4: (2 dc in next st, 1 dc in next 2 sts) 6 times. (24 sts)
Round 5: (2 dc in next st, 1 dc in next 3 sts) 6 times. (30 sts)
Round 6: (2 dc in next st, 1 dc in next 4 sts) 6 times. (36 sts)
Rounds 7-15: 1 dc in each st around. (9 rnds of 36 sts)
Round 16: (dc2tog, 1 dc in next 4 sts) 6 times. (30 sts)
Round 17: (dc2tog, 1 dc in next 3 sts) 6 times. (24 sts)
Fix the safety eyes 11 rows down from the magic ring with 13 sts between each eye. Start stuffing and continue stuffing as you go.
Round 18: (dc2tog, 1 dc in next 2 sts) 6 times. (18 sts)
Round 19: (dc2tog, 1 dc in next st) 6 times. (12 sts)
Round 20: (dc2tog) 6 times. (6 sts)
Fasten off, leaving a tail for sewing.
Using yarn needle, weave the yarn tail through the front ring of each remaining st and pull it tight to close. Using the tail end of yarn from the body, sew the head to the body. (The back of the neck should be sewn onto the head approx 6 rnds away from the head's magic ring.)

TAIL

Using col 1, make a magic ring.
Round 1: 4 dc in magic ring. (4 sts)
Round 2: 1 dc in each st around. (4 sts)
Round 3: 2 dc in next st, 1 dc in each remaining st. (5 sts)
Rounds 4-25: As rnd 2. (27 sts after rnd 25)
Fasten off, leaving a long tail for sewing.
Stuff the tail with fibrefill and sew it to the body as follows:
Place the body on a table in an upright position and pin the tail in place first. If you try to sew the tail on at an angle to the body, you might find that it stops the legs from resting on the ground when you sew them on later.

LEGS (MAKE 2)

Using col 1, make a magic ring.
Round 1: 6 dc in magic ring (6 sts)
Round 2: 2 dc in each st around. (12 sts)
Round 3 (blo): 1 dc in each st around. (12 sts)
Rounds 4-9: 1 dc in each st around. (6 rnds of 12 sts)
Fasten off, leaving a long tail for sewing.

ARMS (MAKE 2)

Using col 1, make a magic ring.
Round 1: 4 dc in magic ring. (4 sts)
Rounds 2-7: 1 dc in each st around. (6 rnds of 4 sts)
Fasten off, leaving a long tail for sewing.

FINGERS (MAKE 2)

Using col 1, make a magic ring.
Round 1: 4 dc in magic ring. (4 sts)
Rounds 2-3: 1 dc in each st around. (2 rnds of 4 sts)
Fasten off, leaving a long tail for sewing.
When both the arms and fingers are complete, sew the finger to the arm so that the end of the arm and the finger are both of equal length. Sew the arms to the body approx 7-8 rows below the point where the head attaches to the body.

TOENAILS

Using col 2, cut a length of yarn about as long as your arm and attach it to the edge of the foot, ch 3, 1 dc back into the same st (one toenail made). *Pull the yarn through two sts to the left for the next toenail, ch 3, 1 dc back into the same st; rep from * once more to make the final toenail. Fasten off, weave in all yarn ends.

NAIL TIPS

Using col 2, cut a short piece of yarn and pull the yarn through a st at the tip of a finger, ch 1, move the hook to a st to the left of the finger, 1 dc, ch 1, pull the yarn through and fasten off. Weave in the yarn ends gently to avoid distorting the ch 1 tip to the nail you just made.

Finishing

First stuff each leg firmly at the bottom, and less firmly at the top so that you can pinch the opening shut, folding it in half. Now find a spot on the side of the dinosaur where you want to attach the leg. Hold the body above a table as far as you want it to stand when all the legs are sewn on. Go down the leg about 3-5 sts until you see the bowed leg finally tighten and line up straight with the side of the body. Fasten off and weave in the yarn end.

Note: To keep legs even you need to attach each leg at the exact same row on the body.

Textured hot water bottle cosy

This pretty, striped hot water bottle cover will make an ideal gift. You could even work it in shades to match a bedroom's decor

Difficulty ★ ★ ★ ★ ★

Skills needed

Joining new yarn
Changing colours
Chain start
Spike stitches
Making eyelets
Blocking

Finished measurements

22cm (8½in) wide x 34cm (13¼in) deep

Hook

5mm (H/8) crochet hook

Tension

17 stitches and 17 rows = 10 x 10cm (4 x 4in) over dc using 5mm (US H/8) hook.
8 stitches and 11 rows = 10 x 10cm (4 x 4in) over five stitch marguerite cluster pattern using 5mm (US H/8) hook.

Yarn

Debbie Bliss Cashmerino Aran
Fibre content: 55% wool, 33% acrylic, 12% cashmere
Ball measurements: 50g/90m/98yd
Colour 1: Mulberry; 1 ball
Colour 2: Ecru; 1 ball

Notions

Tapestry needle

Special stitch patterns

M5C — five stitch marguerite cluster:
Pick up spike loops (by inserting hook and drawing yarn through) inserting hook as follows: into loop which closed previous M5C, under the two threads of last spike loop of previous M5C, into same place as last spike loop of previous M5C, and into next two sts — you now have six loops on hook. Hook yarn and draw yarn through all loops.

Pattern notes

The fabric made with the marguerite stitch pattern will have a tendency to lean towards the right. This is addressed by gently pulling and pinning the work straight during the blocking process (see tutorial on page 78).

Pattern

SIDE (MAKE 2)
With 5mm hook and col 1, ch 38.
Foundation row (WS): 1 dc into 2nd ch from hook ,
1 dc in every ch to end. (37 sts)
Row 1 (col 1): ch 3, make 1 M5C by inserting hook into 2nd and 3rd chain from hook, and then into first
3 sts (to pick up the five spike loops), (1 ch, M5C) to last st, turn.
Row 2: ch 1, 1 dc into loop that closed last M5C, (1 dc into next ch, 1 dc into loop that closed next M5C) across row, ending with 1 dc into each of next 2 ch, turn.
Change to col 2.

Rows 3 and 4 (col 2): As rows 1 and 2.
These four rows set pattern and stripes. Cont in stripes until work measures 30cm (11¾in) ending with row 4 (col 2).
Cont in col 1 only.
Eyelet row (RS): ch 1, 1 dc in 1st dc, (ch 1, skip 1 dc, work 1 dc in next dc) rep to end, turn.
Next row: ch 1, work 1 dc in each dc and each ch gap to end, turn. (37 sts)
Next row: ch 1, dc to end.
Rep last row until work measures 33.5cm (13in).
Change to col 2 and work one more dc row. Fasten off.

Finishing

Weave in ends, pin the pieces to size and shape (see pattern notes). Join base and side seams.
Plait four strands of col 1 and four strands of col 2 together to form a cord and thread through eyelets.

> *"Worked with just two balls of Aran-weight yarn, this cosy cover is an ideal stash buster project"*

SIAN BROWN

After completing a Fashion/Textiles BA, Sian worked for several years as a designer on factory machine knits for suppliers to the main high street retailers. From there she went on to work as a freelance designer on commercial handknits. Then she turned her hand to design for magazines — both knit and crochet. Her book *The Knitted Home* is available now, and she has designed for several other titles.

ALSO BY SIAN:
Traditional tea cosy (p144)

Aran cushion cover

It is possible to get the knitted aran look with a crochet hook. This cushion would look great teamed up with a fluffy throw

Difficulty ★★★★☆

Skills needed

Joining new yarn
Blocking
Joining
Double trebles
Crossed stitches
Post stitches
Cluster stitches (bobbles)
Buttonholes (see page 143)

Finished measurements

Assembled cushion measures 50 x 50cm (30 x 30in)

Hook

4.5mm (US G/7) crochet hook

Yarn

Sublime Extra Fine Merino Worsted
Fibre content: 100% merino wool
Ball measurements: 50g/100m/109yd
Colour: Salty Grey, 010; x 13 balls

Tension (Gauge)

16 stitches and 9 rows = 10 x 310cm (4 x 4in) over treble crochet using 4.5mm (US 7) hook.

18.5 stitches and 13.5 rows = 10 x 10cm (4 x 4in) over Basket Weave Pattern using 4.5mm (US 7) hook.

Notions

50 x 50cm (20 x 20in) cushion pad

Locking stitch markers or safety pins
Tapestry needle
5 x 2.5cm (1in) buttons
Sewing needle and matching thread

Special stitch patterns

C2F

Cross 2 stitches at the front: Skip 1 st, work 1 dtr in front post of next stitch, then work 1 dtr in front post of skipped stitch.

C6F

Cross 6 stitches at the front: Skip 3 stitches, work 1 dtr in front post of each of next 3 stitches, then work 1 dtr in front post of each of 3 skipped stitches beginning with the first skipped stitch.

MB

Work 5 dtr in next stitch, only working each stitch until 1 loop remains for each dtr (6 loops now on the hook), yarn over hook and pull through the 6 loops to form bobble.

BPdtr

Work double treble into the back post.

FPtr

Work double treble into the front post.

Buttonholes

See tutorial on page 143.

Pattern notes

For a firmer edge to the upper back panel, work into the middle loop (or bump) on the back of the chain when working the foundation row.
Stitch counts remain consistent throughout.

Pattern

FRONT

Using 4.5mm hook, ch 87.
Foundation Row: 1 tr into 4th ch from hook (counts as 3 ch and 1 tr), 1 tr into each ch to end, turn. (85 sts)
Row 1 (RS): 3 ch (counts as 1 tr), 1 tr into each of next 4 tr, C2F, 1 tr into each of next 3 tr, (C6F, 1 tr into each of next 3 tr) twice, C2F, 1 tr into each of next 4 tr, MB, 1 tr into each of next 5 tr, MB, 1 tr into each of next 3 tr, MB, 1 tr into each of next 5 tr, MB, 1 tr into each of next 4 tr, C2F, (1 tr into each of next 3 tr, C6F) twice, 1 tr into each of next 3 tr, C2F, 1 tr into each of next 4 tr, 1 tr in third ch of turning ch, turn.
Row 2 (WS): 3 ch (counts as 1 tr), 1 tr into each of next 4 tr, 1 BPdtr into each of next 2 dtr, 1 tr into each of next 3 tr, (1 BPdtr into each of next 6 dtr, 1 tr into each of next 3 tr) twice, 1 BPdtr into each of next 2 dtr, 1 tr into each of next 25 sts (i.e in tr or the top of bobbles made on previous row), 1 BPdtr into each of next 2 dtr, (1 tr into each of next 3 tr, 1 BPdtr into each of next 6 dtr) twice, 1 tr into each of next 3 tr, 1 BPdtr into each of next 2 dtr, 1 tr into each of next 4 tr, 1 tr in 3rd ch of 3 turning chain, turn.
Row 3 (RS): 3 ch (counts as 1 tr), 1 tr into each of next 4 tr, C2F, 1 tr into each of next 3 tr, (C6F, 1 tr into each of next 3 tr) twice, C2F, 1 tr into each of next 4 tr, MB, (1 tr into each of next 7 tr, MB) twice, 1 tr into each of next 4 tr, C2F, (1 tr into each of next 3 tr, C6F) twice, 1 tr into each of next 3 tr, C2F, 1 tr into each of next 4 tr, 1 tr in third ch of turning ch, turn.
Row 4 (WS): Rep Row 2.
Row 5 (RS): 3 ch (counts as 1 tr), 1 tr into each of next 4 tr, C2F, 1 tr into each of next 3 tr, (C6F, 1 tr into each of next 3 tr) twice, C2F, 1 tr into each of next 4 tr, MB, 1 tr into each of next 15 tr, MB, 1 tr into each of next 4 tr, C2F, (1 tr into each of next 3 tr, C6F) twice, 1 tr into each of next 3 tr, C2F, 1 tr into each of next 4 tr, 1 tr in third ch of turning ch, turn.
Row 6 (WS): Rep Row 2.
Row 7 (RS): Rep Row 3.
Row 8 (WS): Rep Row 2.
Row 9 (RS): Rep Row 1.

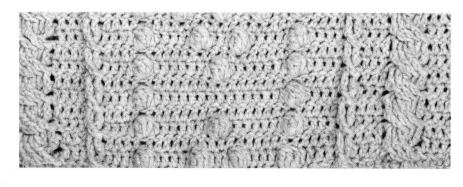

Donna Jones

Donna Jones designs, edits, writes and teaches handknit and crochet. First taught to knit by her mother when she was four years old, she has been surrounded by yarn for as long as she can remember. She firmly believes creative expression is essential for our wellbeing and aims to facilitate this in others. To find more about Donna, visit her website at donnajonesdesigns.co.uk or find her on Instagram @djonesdesigns.

ALSO BY DONNA:

Squares baby blanket (p130)
Lace shell-edged
shawl (p148)
Jumbo rib scarf (p156)

Row 10 (WS): Rep Row 2.
Row 11 (RS): 3 ch (counts as 1 tr), 1 tr into each of next 4 tr, C2F, 1 tr into each of next 3 tr, (C6F, 1 tr into each of next 3 tr) twice, C2F, 1 tr into each of next 4 tr, MB, (1 tr into each of next 3 tr, MB) 4 times, 1 tr into each of next 4 tr, C2F, (1 tr into each of next 3 tr, C6F) twice, 1 tr into each of next 3 tr, C2F, 1 tr into each of next 4 tr, 1 tr in third ch of turning ch, turn.
Row 12 (WS): Rep Row 2.
Rep Rows 1-12 twice more, and then Rows 1-10 once more, working a total of 47 rows, ending with Row 10.
Fasten off.

LOWER BACK PANEL
Using 4.5mm hook, ch 96.
Foundation Row: 1 tr in 4th ch from hook (counts as 3 ch and 1 tr), 1 tr into each ch to end, turn. (94 sts)
Row 1 (RS): 2 ch (counts as 1 htr), *1 FPtr into each of next 4 sts, 1 BPtr into each of next 4 sts; rep for * to last 5 sts, 1 FPtr into each of next 4 sts, 1 tr in top of turning ch, turn.
Row 2 (WS): 2 ch (counts as 1 htr), *1 BPtr into each of next 4 sts, 1 FPtr into each of next 4 sts; rep for * to last 5 sts, 1 BPtr into each of next 4 sts, 1 tr in top of turning ch, turn.
Row 3: As Row 1.
Row 4-5: As Row 2.
Row 6: As Row 1.
Row 7: As Row 2.
Row 8: As Row 1.
Rows 1-8 form Basket Weave Pattern.
Rep Rows 1-8 a further 5 times, and then rep Rows 1-4 once more.
Fasten off.

UPPER BACK PANEL
Using 4.5mm hook, ch 83.
Row 1 (RS): 1 dc in 2nd ch from hook, 1 dc into each ch to end, turn. (82 sts)
Row 2: 1 ch (does not count as dc), 1 dc into each st to end, turn.
Rows 3-6: Rep Row 2 a further 4 times.
Row 7 (Buttonholes): 1 ch (does not count as st), 1 dc into each of next 7 dc, (4 ch, skip next 4 sts, 1 dc into each of next 12 dc) 4 times, 4 ch, skip next 4 sts, 1 dc into each of next 7 dc, turn. (5 buttonholes made)
Row 8: 1 ch (does not count as dc), 1 dc into each of next 7 dc, (4 dc into 4 ch sp, 1 dc into each of next 12 dc) 4 times, 4 dc into 4 ch sp, 1 dc into each of next 7 dc, turn.
Rows 9-12: Rep Row 2 a further 4 times.
Row 13: 3 ch (counts as first 1 tr), 1 tr into

each tr to end, turn.
Rows 14-24: Rep Row 13 a further 11 times.
Fasten off.

Finishing

Weave in ends, pin out to size and block by spraying with a little water to dampen. Allow to dry completely.

Place a marker at each side of Front, approx 19cm from the top edge. Place a marker at each side of Lower Back panel, approx 7cm from the top edge.

With RS facing upwards, lay Front panel flat. Place Upper panel on top of this with WS facing up, ensuring the top edge lines up with the top edge of the front. Now lay the bottom panel on top of both pieces with WS facing up, bottom edge lined up with bottom of from panel, and markers aligned with the markers on the front and upper back — there should be some overlap of the Upper and Lower Back panels. Secure in position with safety pins all around the edge. Sew all around the top, bottom and sides with backstitch.

Turn right side out through the opening on the back. Stitch buttons on Lower Back panel to align with buttonholes.

Place cushion insert inside and fasten with buttons for the final touch.

Buttonholes tutorial

1. When you're ready to begin the designated row for the bottom of the buttonhole, chain (ch) 1 to start the new row. Double crochet (dc) in each of first 3 stitches, and then turn, leaving the remaining stitches of the row unworked.
2. Chain 1 and then double crochet in each stitch across the first half of the buttonhole, *turn.*
3. Repeat Step 2.
4. Fasten off the yarn and, with the right side facing you, skip 1 double crochet and rejoin the yarn on the other side to begin making the second side of the buttonhole.

Remember to rejoin the yarn so that you work in the same direction as the other side; otherwise, you end up with a different stitch pattern. If the first row of the buttonhole row is worked with the right side of your work facing you, make sure that when you rejoin your yarn to work the second side, the right side of your work is also facing you.

1. Chain 1 and double crochet in each stitch across the remainder of the front, *turn.*
2. Work 3 more rows of double crochet across, ending with a wrong side row at the top of the buttonhole.
3. Chain 1, skip the space for the buttonhole, and double crochet in each of the next 3 double crochets on the first side of the buttonhole.

> *"For a firmer edge to the upper back panel, work into the middle loop (or bump) on the back of the chain when working the foundation row"*

Traditional tea cosy

Test your skills and add some retro charm to a teapot

SIAN BROWN

After completing a Fashion/Textiles BA, Sian worked for several years as a designer on factory machine knits for suppliers to the main high street retailers. From there she went on to work as a freelance designer on commercial handknits. Then she turned her hand to design for magazines — both knit and crochet. Her book *The Knitted Home* is available now, and she has designed for several other titles.

Difficulty ★ ★ ★ ☆ ☆

Skills needed

Joining new yarn
Changing colours
Chain start
Flowers
Picot edge
Eyelets

Finished measurements

Width: 21.5cm (8.4 in).
Depth: 18cm (7.08in) (excluding gathered top).

Hook

4mm (G/6) crochet hook
4.5mm (G/7) crochet hook

Yarn

Drops Alaska Aran
Fibre content: 100% wool
Ball measurements: 70m/50g/76yd
Colour 1: Off-white.
Aran weight yarn in the following quantities:
Colour 2: Orange Mix; 82 yards (75m)
Colour 3: Cerise; 82 yards (75m)
Colour 4: Light Olive; 82 yards (75m)
Colour 5: Light Grey Green; 82 yards (75m)
Shown in Drops Nepal, 65% wool, 35% alpaca,
82 yards (50g; 75m) per ball.

Tension (gauge)

16 stitches and 8.5 rows = 10 x 10cm (4 x 4in)
over main pattern using 4.50mm (7) hook.

Notions

Tapestry needle

Pattern

TEA COSY SIDES (MAKE 2)

Using 4mm (G/6) crochet hook and col 1, ch
36.
Row 1 (RS): 1 dc into 2nd ch from hook, 1 dc
into each ch to end, turn. (35 sts)
Row 2: ch 1, 1 dc into each dc to end, turn.
With RS facing work the following:
Main pattern colour sequence:
1 row of each colour in the following order: col
2, col 3, col 4, col 1 and col 5.
Change to col 2 and 4.5mm (G/7) crochet
hook.
Foundation Row (RS, col 2): ch 4 (count as
first tr and ch 1 sp), skip 2 dc, * 3 tr into next
dc, ch 1, skip 3 dc; rep from * to last 4 sts, 3 tr
into next dc, skip 2 dc, 1 tr into dc, fasten off,
DO NOT TURN.
Change to col 3.

Row 1 (RS, col 3): Join with sl st into 3rd ch at
beg of prev row, ch 3 (count as first tr), 2 tr into
first ch sp, * ch 1, 3 tr into next ch sp; rep from
* to last 3 tr and ch sp, ch 1, skip 3 tr, 2 tr into
last ch sp, 1 tr into last tr, fasten off. DO NOT
TURN.
Change to col 4.
Row 2 (RS, col 4): Join with sl st into 3rd ch
at beg of prev row, ch 4 (count as first tr and
ch 1 sp), skip 2 tr, * 3 tr into next ch sp, ch 1;
rep from * to last 3 tr, skip 2 tr, 1 tr into last tr,
fasten off. DO NOT TURN.
These last 2 rows set the pattern ONLY. Rep
these 2 rows 5 times more, AT SAME TIME
rep the colour sequence as stated above, thus
ending with a patt row 2 with col 4.

TOP EDGE WITH EYELETS

Change to 4mm (G/6) crochet hook.
With RS facing and using col 1 only, join with sl
st into 3rd ch at beg of prev row.
Next row: ch 1, dc into same place, 1 dc into
each ch sp and tr of previous row, turn. (35 sts)
Next row: ch 1, 1 dc into each dc to end, turn.
Eyelet row (RS): ch 1, 1 dc into first dc, * ch 1,
skip next dc, 1 dc into each of next 3 dc; rep
from * 7 times more, ch 1, skip next dc, 1 dc
into last dc of row, turn.
Next row: ch 1, 1 dc into each dc and ch sp,
turn. (35 sts)
Next row: ch 1, 1 dc into each dc to end, turn.
Rep last row 3 times more.
Fasten off.

CROCHET FLOWERS (MAKE 2)

Using 4mm (G/6) crochet hook and col 3, make
a magic ring, ch 1 (see p66).
Rnd 1: 10 dc into ring, pull the ring closed, sl st
into first dc of rnd.
Rnd 2: * ch 3, 2 tr into back loop only of next
dc and leaving the last loop of each on hook,

yrh and draw through all loops on hook, ch 3, sl
st into next dc, (petal made), rep from * to end,
working last sl st into base of first ch 3 of round
(total 5 petals made).
Fasten off.

Finishing

First, sew up sides of tea cosy leaving space open
for spout and handle.

PICOT EDGING

With RS facing and using 4mm (G/6) hook with col
2, join with a sl st into dc of previous row at either
top side seam.
Picot Row: 1 dc into same place as sl st, 1 dc into
next dc, * ch 3, sl st into 3rd ch from hook (picot
made),1 dc into each of next 3 dc; rep from * to last
2 dc, ch 3, sl st into 3rd ch from hook, 1 dc into
each of last 2 dc, sl st into first dc of rnd.
Fasten off.

CORD

Using 4mm (G/6) crochet hook and col 5 make a
chain 60cm long for the drawstring. Thread crochet
cord through the eyelets, beginning and ending at
the centre of the side of the cosy. Sew 1 flower to
each end of cord using the yarn left at the ends.
Pull cord tight to fit your teapot.

Spring flower brooch

Create this beautiful, and simple, spring brooch in whatever colours you like to add a flourish of colour to any outfit

Difficulty ★ ★ ☆ ☆ ☆

Skills needed

Magic loop start
Working in the round
Flowers

Finished measurements

Each flower measures 9cm across

Hook

4mm (US G/6) crochet hook

Tension

Tension is not critical for this project.

Yarn

DMC Woolly
Fibre content: 100% merino wool
Ball measurements: 125m/136yds
Colour 1: Orange Shade 10 (oddment)
Colour 2: Cream Shade 03 (oddment)
Colour 3: Lime Green Shade 81 (oddment)

Notions

Wool needle
Brooch back or safety pin
Sewing needle and thread

Pattern

FLOWER

With 4mm hook and col 1, make a magic loop.
Round 1: ch 2 (not counted as a st), 16 htr into magic loop, miss skip the beginning ch 2 and sl st into first htr to join (16 sts). Pull the magic ring closed.

Round 2: *ch 2, skip next st, sl st in next st; rep from * another 7 times, working the last sl st into the base of the first ch 2 (8 sl st and 8 ch 2 spaces).
Round 3: (1 dc, 1 tr, 2 dtr, 1 tr, 1 dc) all into each ch 2 space (beneath the 8 sl st) around, sl st into first dc to join (8 petals).
Round 4: *ch 4, 1 dc in the space between the next 2 petals, then lift the chain over the petal so that it sits behind it; rep from * around, sl st into the base of the beginning ch 4, cut yarn and fasten off. Make sure that all of the ch 4 loops are sitting behind a petal (8 x ch 4 loops behind petals).
Round 5: Join col 2 with sl st to any ch 4 loop. ch 1 (not counted as a st), (1 dc, 1 tr, 3 dtr, 1 tr, 1 dc) all into the same ch 4

space, (1 dc, 1 tr, 3 dtr, 1 tr, 1 dc) into each remaining ch 4 space around, sl st to beginning ch 1 (8 petals).
Round 6: Repeat Round 4. Cut yarn and fasten off.
Round 7: Join col 3 with a sl st to any ch 4 loop. ch 1 (not counted as a st), (1 dc, 1 tr, 4 dtr, 1 tr, 1 dc) all into the same ch 4 space, (1 dc, 1 tr, 4 dtr, 1 tr, 1 dc) into each remaining ch 4 space around. Cut yarn and fasten off. Weave all ends into wrong side of flower and trim.

CENTRE:

With 4mm hook and col 2 or col 3, make a magic loop.
Round 1: ch 1 (not counted as a st), 6 dc into magic loop, sl st to first dc to join (6 sts). sl st into next st and fasten off. Make a knot in the centre of a short length of contrast yarn and thread through the centre. Sew to the front of flower.

Finishing

Sew a brooch back to the flower. Make as many flowers as you like using a different order of colours for each round of petals.

> *"Cut yarn and fasten off. Weave all ends into wrong side of flower and trim"*

LYNNE ROWE

Lynne Rowe is a freelance knit and crochet designer, technical editor, craft author, tutor, blogger and podcaster from Cheshire.
To read more about Lynne's crochet adventures, read her blog at www.thewoolnest.blogspot.co.uk.

ALSO BY LYNNE:
Cosy alpaca mittens (p152)

Donna Jones

Donna Jones designs, edits, writes and teaches handknit and crochet. First taught to knit by her mother when she was four years old, she has been surrounded by yarn for as long as she can remember. She firmly believes creative expression is essential for our wellbeing and aims to facilitate this in others. To find more about Donna, visit her website at donnajonesdesigns.co.uk or find her on Instagram @djonesdesigns.

ALSO BY DONNA:

Squares baby blanket (p130)
Aran cushion cover (p140)
Jumbo rib scarf (p156)

Lacy shell-edged shawl

When the weather turns cooler, a shawl is the perfect garment to wear on days when a coat is too much

Difficulty ★★★☆☆

Skills needed

Joining new yarn
Increasing
Magic ring
Blocking
Shell, Fans & V stitches

Finished measurements

The finished shawl measures 160cm (63in) along the top edge and 81cm (31¾ in) deep measured from the top centre to the bottom tip of shawl, after blocking

Hook

5mm (US H/8) crochet hook

Yarn

Mirasol Sulka Nina (DK)
Fibre content: 60% extra fine merino, 20% baby alpaca, 20% mulberry silk
Ball measurements: 50g/150m/164yd
Total meterage/yardage for project: 870m/951yd
Colour: Coral, 7113; 6 balls

Tension (Gauge)

15 sts and 20 rows = 10 x 10cm (4 x 4in) over treble stitch using 5mm (US H/8) crochet hook, or size required to obtain correct tension.

Notions

Tapestry needle

Pattern notes

Shawl is worked from the top downwards, forming a fabric which resembles two triangles that lie each side of a central 'spine'.

> *"Shawl is worked from the top downwards, forming a fabric which resembles two triangles"*

Check you have the correct number of stitches at the end of each row or half row — spotting a mistake earlier on will save you a lot of frustration.

Pattern

MAIN SECTION

Using 5mm hook, make a magic ring (see tutorial on page 66), then work 3 ch (counts as 1 tr), 2 tr, 2 ch, 3 tr into the ring, pull ring closed, turn. (6 sts — 2 groups of 3 tr)

Row 1 (inc): 3 ch (counts as 1 tr), 2 tr into tr at base of ch, 1 tr into each tr to ch sp, (2 tr, 2 ch, 2 tr) all into ch sp, 1 tr into each tr to last st, 3 tr into 3rd of 3 ch, turn. (14 sts — 2 groups of 7 tr)

Row 2 (inc): 3 ch (counts as 1 tr), 1 tr into tr at base of ch, 1 tr into each tr to ch sp, (2 tr, 2 ch, 2 tr) all into next ch sp, 1 tr into each tr to last st, 2 tr into 3rd of 3 ch, turn. (20 sts - 2 groups of 10 tr)

Repeat Row 2 for 34 rows. Each repeated row increases your stitch count by 6. (You should have a total of 224 sts — 2 groups of 112 tr).

Do not fasten off.

BORDER — LEAF PATTERN

Commence leaf pattern, as follows:

Row 1: ch 3 (counts as 1 tr), 3 tr in st at base of ch, miss 2 tr, 1 dc in next tr, [miss 2 tr, 7 tr in next tr, miss 2 tr, 1 dc in next tr] 18 times, (2 tr, 2 ch, 2 tr) all in 2-ch sp, 1 dc in next tr, miss 2 tr, [7 tr in next tr, miss 2 tr, 1 dc in next tr, miss 2 tr] 18 times, 4 tr in 3rd of 3 ch, turn.

(1 half shell, and 18 full shells on each side of the centre (2 tr, 2 ch, and 2 tr) stitches)

Row 2 (inc): Make 3 ch (counts as 1 tr), 1 tr in st at base of ch (1 st increased), 3 ch, miss 3 tr, 1 tr in next dc, [3 ch, miss 3 tr, 1 tr in next tr, 3 ch, miss 3 tr, 1 tr in next dc] to 2 tr before 2-ch sp, 2 ch, miss 2 tr (2 tr, 2 ch, 2 tr) in 2-ch sp, 2 ch, miss 2 tr, [1 tr in next dc, 3 ch, miss 3 tr, 1 tr in next tr, 3 ch, miss 3 tr]

to last dc, 1 tr in next dc, 3 ch, miss 3 tr, 2 tr in 3rd of 3 ch (1 st increased), turn.

Row 3 (inc): Make 1 ch (does not count as a st), 1 dc in st at base of ch, 1 ch (1 st increased), [1 dc in next tr, 3 ch] to 2 tr before 2-ch sp, miss 2 ch and 1 tr, 1 dc in next tr, (2 dc, 2 ch, 2 dc) all in centre 2-ch sp, 1 dc in next tr, 3 ch, miss 1 tr and 2 ch, 1 dc in next tr, [3 ch, 1 dc in next tr] to last st, 1 ch, (1 st increased) 1 dc in 3rd of ch 3, turn.

Row 4 (inc): Make 3 ch (counts as 1 tr), 3 tr in st at base of ch (1 st increased), 1 dc in next dc, [7 tr in next dc, 1 dc in next dc] to 3 dc before 2-ch sp, miss 2 dc, 4 tr in next dc, (2 tr, 2 ch, 2 tr) all in centre 2-ch sp, 4 tr in next dc, miss 2 dc and 3 ch, 1 dc in next dc, [7 tr in next dc, 1 dc in next dc] to last dc, 4 tr in next dc 1 st increased), turn.

(1 half shell, 19 full shells and another half shell on each side of the centre (2 tr, 2 ch, 2 tr) stitches)

Rows 5-13: Rep Rows 2-4, 3 times.

(1 half shell, 23 full shells and another half shell on each side of the centre (2 tr, 2 ch, 2 tr) stitches).

COMMENCE FAN EDGING

Row 14: ch 3 (counts as 1 tr), miss 4 tr, V st in next dc, [5 ch, miss 7 tr, V st in next dc] to 6 tr before 2-ch sp, 5 ch, miss 6 tr, (2 tr, 2 ch, 2 tr) all in 2 ch sp, 2 ch, miss 6 tr, V st in next dc, [5 ch, miss 7 tr, V st in next dc] to last 4 tr, 3 ch, ss to top of 3 turning ch from 12th row, turn.

Row 15: ch 1, 1 dc in st at base of ch, tr in 1-ch sp at centre of next V st, [working over next 5 ch on prev row so as to enclose it, work 1 dc in 4th tr of next shell from row 13, 9 tr in 1-ch sp at centre of next V st] to last 2 tr before centre 2-ch sp, 7 tr in next tr, miss 1 tr, (2 tr, 2 ch, 2 tr) all in 2-ch sp, 7 tr in next tr, miss 1 tr, work 1 dc in 1st tr of 4-tr shell from row 13, [9 tr in 1-ch sp at centre of next V st, work 1 dc in 4th tr of shell from row 13 as before] to last V st, 9 tr in 1-ch sp at centre of next V st, 1 dc in 1st of 3 ch from beg of prev row, turn.

Row 16: ch 4 and 1 tr in st at base of ch, (counts as V st), [5 ch, miss 9 tr, V st in next dc] ending in last dc before centre 2-ch sp, 5

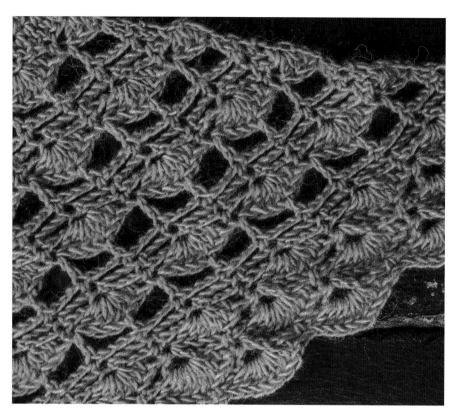

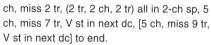

ch, miss 2 tr, (2 tr, 2 ch, 2 tr) all in 2-ch sp, 5 ch, miss 7 tr, V st in next dc, [5 ch, miss 9 tr, V st in next dc] to end.

Row 17: ch 3 (counts as 1 tr), 4 tr in 1-ch sp at centre of next V st, [working over next 5 ch on prev row so as to enclose it, work 1 dc in 5th tr of next shell from row 15, 9 tr in 1-ch sp at centre of next V st] to last 2 tr before centre 2-ch sp, 7 tr in next tr, miss 1 tr, (2 tr, 2 ch, 2 tr) all in 2-ch sp, 7 tr in next tr, miss 1 tr, work 1 dc in 1st tr of 4-tr shell from row 13, [9 tr in 1-ch sp at centre of next V st, work 1 dc in 4th tr of shell from row 13 as before] to last V st, 9 tr in 1-ch sp at centre of next V st, 5 tr in 1-ch sp at centre of next V st.

Fasten off.

Finishing

Darn in ends. Gently spray with water and lay flat or 'block' (see pages 76-79 for tutorials), pinning it out flat and gently easing in shape as per finished dimensions and so that the top edge lies straight and the edging is pulled out slightly to emphasise the shell pattern.

Cosy alpaca mittens

When there's a chill in the air, but you still want to be able to use your fingers for texting or crocheting, these mitts will keep your hands warm

Difficulty ★★☆☆☆

Skills needed

Half treble crochet
Working in the round
Front post treble
Back post treble

Finished measurements

18cm long x 20cm around

Hook

4mm (US G/6) crochet hook

Tension

18 htr in the round measure 10cm.

Yarn

The Big Scary Bear: 100% British Alpaca
Content of yarn: 100% alpaca
Yarn Measurements: 50g/100m/109yd
Total meterage/yardage: 100g/200m/118yd
Colour 1: Pebble x 1 ball
Colour 2: Cream x 1 ball

Notions

Wool needle

Pattern notes

For the Main Mitten pattern, each round is joined and work is turned ready for the next round.
The beginning 2 ch of each round is not counted as a stitch. It is used to help create an invisible join.
When joining each round, skip the beginning 2 ch and sl st to top of first htr.
The first stitch of each round is worked in the same st at the base of the beginning 2 ch.

Pattern

MITTENS (MAKE 2)

Starting at the top of the mitten, with 4mm hook and col 1, ch 34, sl st into first ch to join into a ring.
Round 1 (RS): ch 2 (not counted as a st here and throughout), 1 htr in same st at base of ch 2, 1 htr in each st around, sl st into top of first htr to join, changing to col 2, turn (34 sts).
Round 2: ch 2, 1 htr in same st at base of ch 2, 1 htr in each st around, sl st into top of first htr to join, turn.
Round 3: ch 2, 1 htr in same st at base of ch 2, 1 htr in each st around, sl st into top of first htr to join, changing to col 1, turn. Cut col 2.
Rounds 4-6: Rep round 2.
Round 7: ch 2, 1 htr in same st at base of ch 2, 1 htr in each of next 16 sts, 2 htr in next st, 1 htr in each of next 16 sts around, sl st into top of first htr to join, turn (35 sts).
Round 8: ch 2, 1 htr in same st at base of ch 2, 1 htr in each of next 13 sts, ch 7, skip next 7 sts, 1 htr in each of next 14 sts, sl st into top of first htr to join, turn (28 htr and 7 ch).
Round 9: ch 2, 1 htr in same st at base of ch 2, 1 htr in each of next 13 sts, 1 htr in each of next 7 ch, 1 htr in each of next 14 sts, sl st into top of first htr to join, turn (35 sts).
Rounds 10-12: Rep round 2.
Round 13: ch 2, 1 htr in same st at base of ch 2, 1 htr in each of next 16 sts, htr2tog, 1 htr in each of next 17 sts around, sl st into top of first htr to join, turn (34 sts).
Rounds 14-18: Rep round 2.
Round 19: ch 3 (counts a 1 FPtr), 1 BPtr in next st, *1 FPtr in next st, 1 BPtr in next st; rep from * around, sl st into top of beginning 3 ch (do not turn).
Round 20-23: Rep Round 19, changing to col 2 on sl st of round 23.
Rounds 24-25: In col 2, rep round 19. Fasten off.

TOP EDGE

Rejoin col 2 to any st around top edge.
Round 26: ch 2 (not counted as st), 1 htr in each st to end, sl st into top of first htr to join (34 sts).
Rounds 27-28: Repeat Round 19 of Main Mittens. Fasten off.

Finishing

Weave in ends to WS and trim.
Make second mitten.

LYNNE ROWE

Lynne Rowe is a freelance knit and crochet designer, technical editor, craft author, tutor, blogger and podcaster from Cheshire.
To read more about Lynne's crochet adventures, read her blog at www.thewoolnest.blogspot.co.uk.

ALSO BY LYNNE:
Spring flower brooch (p146)

Honeycomb belle hat

This cute hat uses a bobble stitch to create a thicker fabric that will keep your head nice and warm. Top it off with a big pompom for an on-trend look

Difficulty ★ ★ ★ ☆ ☆

Skills needed

Working in the round
Making bobbles
Making a pompom

Finished measurements

The hat stretches to fit average female head measuring 51cm (20in)
Actual finished measurements: 44cm (17¼in) around brim, 25.5cm (10in) from crown to edge of brim.

Hook

12 mm (US O/17) crochet hook

Tension

7.5 stitches and 6 rows = 10 x 10cm (4 x 4in) over honeycomb puff pattern using 12mm (US O/17) hook.

Yarn

Debbie Bliss Roma (Super chunky)
Fibre content: 70% wool, 30%
Ball measurements: 100g/80m/87yd
Colour 1: Coral, 017; 1 ball
Colour 2: Citrus, 08; 1 ball

Notions

1 stitch marker
Large-eyed tapestry needle/bodkin
65mm pompom maker (optional)
Sharp scissors

Special stitch patterns

Honeycomb puff pattern
Consists of dc and bobbles made by working 5 treble sts together.

Half treble rib
A variation of half treble stitch, where the stitches are worked by inserting your hook into the loop directly below the top loop that you would normally work into.

Pattern

RIB BRIM
Using 12 mm hook and col 1, ch 6.
Row 1: Skip ch 2 (does not count as st), 1 htr into every ch, to end, turn. (4 sts)
Row 2: ch 2, 1 htr into loop directly below top loops of each htr to end, turn.
Rep row 2 until rib measures approx 44cm (17¼in).

MAIN BODY AND CROWN
Turn work clockwise so that long edge is facing upwards, work 33 dc sts evenly across top of rib, and join to work in the round with a sl st into top of first dc made.
Place stitch marker to indicate beg/end of each rnd.
Honeycomb Puff Stitch
Round 1: ch 1, 1 dc into base of ch, 1 dc in next dc, *tr5tog, 1 dc in next 2 dc; rep from * to last dc, t5tog, sl st into first dc made.
Round 2: ch 1, 1 dc into base of ch, 1 dc in next dc, * 1 dc in top of tr5tog, 1 dc in next 2 dc; rep from * to last st, 1 dc in top of tr5tog, sl st into first dc made.
Round 3: ch 1, *tr5tog in next dc, 1 dc in next 2 dc; rep from * to end, sl st in top of first tr5tog made.
Round 4: ch 1, *1 dc in top of tr5tog, 1 dc in next 2 dc; rep from * to end, sl st into first dc made.
Rounds 5-7: Rep Rnds 1-3.
Change to col 2.
Round 8 (Colour 2): Rep Rnd 4.
Round 9: Rep Rnd 1.
Round 10 (dec): ch 1, 1 dc in base of ch, *skip 1 dc, 1dc in next 2 dc; rep from * to last 2 sts, skip 1 dc, 1 dc in next st, sl st into first dc made. (22 sts)
Round 11: ch 1, *tr5tog in next dc, 1 dc in next dc; rep from * to end, sl st into first tr5tog made.
Round 12: ch 1, *1 dc in top of tr5tog, 1dc in next dc; rep from * to end sl st into first dc made.
Round 13 (dec): ch 1, 1 dc in base ch, *skip 1 dc, 1 dc in next dc; rep from * to last dc, skip 1 dc, sl st into first dc made. (11 sts)

EMMA WRIGHT

Emma is a designer with a passion for British fashion, flowers and her home county of Yorkshire.
See more from her at:
www.emmaknitted.co.uk
Ravelry username: emmaknitsjumpers
Twitter: @Emmaknitted
Instagram: @Emmaknitted

Round 14 (dec): ch 1, 1 dc in base, *skip 1, 1 dc in next dc; rep from * to last 2 dc, skip 2 dc, sl st into first dc made. (5 sts)
Fasten off.
Use a running stitch around the top of the crown, pull gently to drawn in and close.

Finishing

Join rib seam neatly and fasten off any loose ends.
Using col 2 make a 65mm pompom and join to centre of crown.

> *"The ribbed hem is stretchy so the hat will fit snugly to your head while out on blustery winter walks"*

Jumbo rib scarf

This is an ideal project to make if you're new to crochet as the thick yarn and large hook will mean that you'll complete it in no time

Difficulty ★ ★ ☆ ☆ ☆

Skills needed

Joining new yarn
Blocking
Post stitches
Fringe

Finished measurements

Scarf measures 24cm (9½in) wide and 210cm (82¾in) long, excluding fringe.

Hook

12mm (US O/17) crochet hook

Tension

7 stitches and 6 rows = 10 x 10cm (4 x 4in) over rib pattern using 12mm (US O/17) hook.

Yarn

Hayfield Super Chunky with Wool
Fibre content: 80% acrylic, 20% wool
Ball measurements: 100g/72m/79yd
Total meterage/yardage for project: 504m/553yd
Colour: Poole, 56; 7 balls

Notions

Large-eyed tapestry needle/bodkin
Sharp scissors

Pattern notes

You can easily make this longer or shorter by using more or fewer balls of yarn.

Cut your tassels to your desired length before starting to crochet your scarf. This way you will be able to work your scarf as long as possible by continuing until you have no yarn remaining.

Don't be tempted to skip the blocking stage — it makes a considerable difference to the way that your finished scarf sits when worn and is well worth the effort

Pattern

Cut 64 lengths of yarn each measuring 60cm long and set aside for the fringe.

MAKE SCARF
Using 12mm hook, ch 19.
Foundation Row: 1 tr into 4th ch from hook (counts as 2 tr), 1 tr into every ch to end, turn. (17 sts)

Row 1 (RS): ch 2 (counts as 1 st), miss st at base of ch, (1 FPtr into next tr, 1 BPtr into next tr) 7 times, 1 FPtr into next tr, 1 tr into 3rd of ch 3, turn.
Row 2: ch 2 (counts as 1 st), miss st at base of ch, (1 BPtr into next tr, 1 FPtr into next tr) 7 times, 1 BPtr into next tr, 1 tr into 3rd of ch 3, turn.

These 2 rows form rib pattern. Repeat these 2 rows until work measures 210cm (82¾in), or your desired length.
Fasten off.

MAKE FRINGE, see tutorial on pages 112-113. Holding 2 of your pre-cut tassel lengths together, fold in half. With right side facing, and spacing tassels evenly as you work, insert your crochet hook from back to the front through the short edge of scarf. Hook the midpoint of the folded fringe strands and draw the loop through the edge. Pull the ends through the loop and tighten.

Continue adding tassels in this way until all 16 have been made. Repeat for the other end of the scarf. Trim with scissors to straighten the edge of the fringe.

Finishing

Block the scarf by pinning it out flat without stretching it, spray liberally with cool water to moisten, gently patting the water into the crochet and leave to dry completely before unpinning.

> *"Cut your tassels to your desired length before starting to crochet"*

Donna Jones

Donna Jones designs, edits, writes and teaches handknit and crochet. First taught to knit by her mother when she was four years old, she has been surrounded by yarn for as long as she can remember. She firmly believes creative expression is essential for our wellbeing and aims to facilitate this in others. To find more about Donna, visit her website at donnajonesdesigns.co.uk or find her on Instagram @djonesdesigns.

ALSO BY DONNA:

Squares baby blanket (p130)
Aran cushion cover (p140)
Lace shell-edged shawl (p148)

Glossary

All of the key terminology you need to learn to follow patterns and get to grips with the skills and techniques you need for crochet

asterisk*
A symbol used to mark a point in a pattern row, usually at the beginning of a set of repeated instructions.

back loop (BL) only
A method of crocheting in which you work into only the back loop of a stitch instead of both loops.

back post (BP) stitches
Textured stitches worked from the back around the post of the stitch below.

ball band
The paper wrapper around a ball of yarn that contains information such as fibre content, amount/length of yarn, weight, colour and dye lot.

block
A finishing technique that uses moisture to set stitches and shape pieces to their final measurements.

blocking wire
A long, straight wire used to hold the edges of crochet pieces straight during blocking, most often for lace.

bobble
A crochet stitch that stands out from the fabric, formed from several incomplete tall stitches joined at the top and bottom.

Block

brackets [ ]
Symbols used to surround a set of grouped instructions, often used to indicate repeats.

chain (ch)
A simple crochet stitch that often forms the foundation that other stitches are worked into.

chain space (ch-sp)
A gap formed beneath one or more chain stitches, usually worked into instead of into the individual chain(s).

chainless foundation
A stretchy foundation plus first row of stitches that are made in one step

chainless foundation stitches
Stitches that have an extra chain at the bottom so they can be worked into without first crocheting a foundation chain.

chart
A visual depiction of a crochet pattern that uses symbols to represent stitches.

cluster
A combination stitch formed from several incomplete tall stitches joined together at the top.

contrast colour (CC)
A yarn colour used as an accent to the project's main colour.

crochet hook
The tool used to form all crochet stitches.

crossed stitches
Two or more tall stitches that are crossed, one in front of the other, to create an X shape.

decrease (dec)
A shaping technique in which you reduce the number of stitches in your work.

double crochet
The most basic crochet stitch.

double treble crochet (dtr)
A basic crochet stitch three times as tall as a double crochet stitch.

drape
The way in which your crocheted fabric hangs; how stiff or flowing it feels.

draw up a loop
To pull up a loop of yarn through a stitch or space after inserting your hook into that stitch or space.

fan
A group of several tall stitches crocheted into the same base stitch and usually separated by chains to form a fan shape.

fasten off
To lock the final stitch with the yarn end so the crocheted work cannot unravel.

fasten on
To draw up a loop of new yarn through a stitch in preparation to begin crocheting.

foundation chain
A base chain into which most crochet is worked (unless worked in the round).

foundation stitches, chainless
See chainless foundation stitches.

fringe
A decorative edging made from strands of yarn knotted along the edge.

frog
To unravel your crochet work by removing your hook and pulling the working yarn.

front loop (FL) only
A method in which you work into only the front loop of a stitch instead of both loops.

front post (FP) stitches
Textured stitches worked from the front around the post of the stitch below.

gauge (tension)
See tension.

half treble crochet
A basic stitch halfway between the height of a double and treble crochet stitch.

Tension (gauge)

increase (inc)
A shaping technique in which you add extra stitches to your work.

invisible finish
A method of finishing a round or edging so the join is not visible.

knife grip
An overhand method of holding a crochet hook, similar to holding a knife.

linked stitch
A variation of any standard tall stitch that links the stitch to its neighbour partway up the post to eliminate the gaps between stitches and form a solid fabric.

magic ring
A technique to begin working in the round without leaving a hole in the centre by crocheting over an adjustable loop.

main colour (MC)
The predominant yarn colour of a project.

mattress stitch
A stitch to sew a seam that forms an almost invisible join on the right side of the work and a ridged seam on the wrong side.

motif
A crocheted shape usually worked in the round as a geometric shape and combined with other motifs into larger pieces.

parentheses ( )
Symbols used in crochet patterns to surround a set of grouped instructions, often used to indicate repeats.

pencil grip
An underhand method of holding a crochet hook, similar to holding a pencil.

picot
A tiny loop of chain stitches that sits on top of a stitch and creates a small round or pointed shape.

popcorn
A combination crochet stitch that stands out dramatically from the fabric formed from several tall stitches pulled together by a chain stitch.

post
The main vertical stem of a stitch.

post stitch
A stitch formed by crocheting around the post of the stitch in the row or round below, so the stitch sits in front of (or behind) the surface of the fabric.

puff stitch
A combination crochet stitch that forms a smooth, puffy shape created from several incomplete half treble crochet stitches that are joined at the top and bottom.

repeat (rep)
To replicate a series of crochet instructions; one instance of the duplicated instructions.

reverse double crochet
A variation of double crochet that is worked backwards (left to right) around the edge of a piece, producing a corded edging.

right side (RS)
The side of a crocheted piece that's visible.

rip back
To unravel your crochet work.

round (rnd)
A line of stitches worked around a circular crocheted piece.

row
A line of stitches worked across a flat crocheted piece.

shell
A group of several tall stitches, crocheted into the same base stitch, that spread out at the top into a shell shape.

skip (sk)
To pass over a stitch or stitches.

slip knot
A knot that can be tightened by pulling one end of the yarn; used for attaching the yarn to the hook to begin crocheting.

slip stitch (sl st or ss)
A stitch with no height primarily used to join rounds and stitches to move the hook and yarn into a new position.

space (sp)
A gap formed between or beneath stitches, often seen in lace patterns.

spike stich
A stitch worked around existing stitches to extend down to one or more rows below, creating a long vertical spike.

stitch (st)
A group of one or more loops of yarn pulled through each other in a specific order until only one loop remains on the crochet hook.

stitch diagram
A map of a crochet or stitch pattern, where each stitch represented by a symbol.

stitch marker
A small tool you can slide into a crochet stitch or between stitches to mark a position.

swatch
A crocheted sample of a stitch pattern large enough to measure the tension (gauge) and test the pattern with a specific hook and yarn.

tail
A short length of unworked yarn left at the start or end of a piece.

tension (gauge)
A measure of how many stitches and rows fit into a certain length of crocheted fabric, usually 10 centimetres (4 inches), that indicates the size of each stitch.

together (tog)
A shaping technique in which you work two or more stitches into one to reduce the number of stitches.

treble crochet (tr)
A basic stitch twice as tall as a double crochet.

turning chain (t-ch)
A chain made at the start of a row to bring your hook and yarn up to the height of the next row.

V
The two loops at the top of each stitch that from a sideways V shape; standard crochet stitches are worked into both these loops.

V stitch
A group of two tall stitches crocheted into the same base stitch and separated by one or more chains, forming a V shape.

weave in
A method used to secure and hide the yarn tails by stitching them through your crocheted stitches.

whip stitch
A simple stitch to sew a seam by inserting the needle through the edge of both crocheted pieces at once to form each stitch.

working in the round
Crocheting in a circle instead of back and forward in straight rows.

working loop
The single loop that remains on your hook after completing a crochet stitch.

wrong side (WS)
The side of a crocheted piece that will be hidden; the inside or back.

Working in the round

yardage
A length of yarn, usually expressed as an estimate of the amount of yarn required for a project.

yarn needle
A wide, blunt-tipped needle with an eye large enough for the yarn to pass through that's used for stitching crocheted pieces together and weaving in ends.

yarn over (yo)
To pass the yarn over the hook so the yarn is caught in the throat of the hook.

yarn tail
See tail.

yarn weight
The thickness of the yarn (not the weight of a ball or yarn).

TOP TIP
Use a yarn needle instead of a hook to weave the ends back through a project once complete. They will be more secure and less likely to unravel.

Abbreviations

UK stitch name	Abbreviation	Symbol	Description
back loop	**BL**	X	The loop furthest from you at the top of the stitch.
back post double crochet	**BPdc**	T	Yarn over, insert the hook from the back to the front, then to the back around the post of the next stitch, yarn over and draw up a loop, (yarn over and draw through two loops) twice.
chain(s)	**ch(s)**	O	Yarn over and draw through the loop on the hook.
chain space(s)	**ch-sp(s)**		The space beneath one or more chains.
double crochet	**dc**	X or +	Insert the hook into the next stitch and draw up a loop, yarn over and draw through both loops on the hook.
double crochet 2 together	**dc2tog**	XX	(Insert the hook into the next stitch and draw up a loop) twice, yarn over and draw through all three loops on the hook.
double treble crochet	**dtr**	‡	Yarn over twice, insert the hook into the next stitch and draw up a loop, (yarn over and draw through two loops on the hook) three times.
front loop	**FL**	X	The loop closest to you at the top of the stitch.
front post treble crochet	**FPtr**	T	Yarn over, insert the hook from the front to the back to the front around the post of the next stitch, yarn over and draw up a loop, (yarn over and draw through two loops) twice.
half treble crochet	**htr**	T	Yarn over, insert the hook into the next stitch and draw up a loop, yarn over and draw through all three loops on the hook.
repeat	**rep**		Replicate a series of given instructions.
skip	**sk**		Pass over a stitch or stitches — do not work into it.
slip stitch	**sl st or ss**	● or ●	Insert the hook into the next stitch, draw up a loop through the stitch and the loop on the hook.
stitch(es)	**st(s)**		A group of one or more loops of yarn pulled through each other in a specified order until only 1 remains on the crochet hook.
treble crochet	**tr**	T	Yarn over, insert the hook into the next stitch and draw up a loop, (yarn over and draw through two loops on the hook) twice.
treble crochet 2 together	**tr2tog**	A	(Yarn over, insert the hook into the next stitch and draw up a loop, yarn over and draw through two loops on the hook) twice, yarn over and draw through all three loops on the hook.
turning chain	**t-ch**		The chain made at the start of a row to bring your hook and yarn up to the height of the next row.
yarn over	**yo**		Pass the yarn over the hook so the yarn is caught in the throat of the hook.